**LIVING STUDIES**
is a series of high quality
Christian books, both timely
and relevant to today's
problems and challenges. □ In addition to
being some of the best in Christian reading, books in the LIVING STUDIES SERIES
have a dual purpose, being specially designed for small group Bible studies, mid-
week services, adult vacation Bible school,
or as adult Sunday school elective studies.
□ A separate Leader's Guide, designed for
easy out-of-class preparation, makes any lay
person into an interesting and capable discussion leader. Books and Leader's Guides
(some for six sessions, most for thirteen sessions) are available at your Christian book-
store or write Tyndale House Publishers,
Box 80, Wheaton IL 60189.

D1461966

Other books by J. Sidlow Baxter:

Explore the Book
The Strategic Grasp of the Bible
His Part and Ours
Going Deeper
Awake, My Heart
Does God Still Guide?
Mark These Men
Studies in Problem Texts
God So Loved
A New Call to Holiness
His Deeper Work in Us
Our High Calling

The Master Theme of the Bible

PART 1: THE DOCTRINE OF THE LAMB

J · SIDLOW BAXTER

LIVING STUDIES
Tyndale House Publishers, Inc.
Wheaton, Illinois

First printing, Living Studies edition, November 1985
Library of Congress Catalog Card Number 85-51470
ISBN 0-8423-4187-0
Copyright © 1973 by J. Sidlow Baxter
Printed in the United States of America

CONTENTS

FOREWORD

Readers of this book should realize right from the beginning that
the chapters, although they may without presumption be called Bible
studies, are not so in an academic or professionally theological sense.
They are meant for the general public and the average reader. I
believe, however, that such studies do not necessarily lose thereby
any basic worth which they may have. Neither our Lord himself nor
any of his apostles (except Paul) was an academician or specialist
theologian. The public always needs the general practitioner as well
as the specialist. Often he is far better understood.

Further, these chapters now reproduce in print spoken studies used
at Bible conferences, and they largely retain their original form. Here
and there they become conversational rather than merely declarative,
but that suits my own disposition better, and, I think, brings them
closer to most readers. In both the preaching and the writing of these
reflections, the subject has set my own heart singing with new love
and gratitude to our inexpressibly glorious Savior-King, and my
longing is that at least some other hearts may be moved to love and
prize him the more earnestly through the reading of this book.

J. SIDLOW BAXTER
Santa Barbara, California

THE DOCTRINE OF THE LAMB

CHAPTER ONE

THE REVELATION OF THE LAMB

None other Lamb,
None other Name,
None other hope in heav'n or earth or sea;
None other hiding place from guilt and shame:
None beside Thee.

> — *HARRIET BEECHER STOWE*

Do not forget that the Atonement was made
by God, and not simply to God. The initiative
is with God. Then why should we preach
God's reconciliation almost entirely from man's
side, without realizing the Divine initiative
as an act of God's self-reconciliation, timeless,
eternal, in the "Lamb slain from the foundation
of the world"?

> — *HENRY C. MABIE*

OUR BIBLE IS a collection of humanly written documents. That does not mean, however, that it is merely a literary miscellany. There is a basic unity about the documents of the Bible which forms them into one, homogeneous whole, thus making the Bible a *book*.

In many ways the Bible is the most *human* book ever written. But it claims to be much more than that. In its various parts it claims to be nothing less than the written Word of God, given by direct and inerrant divine inspiration through chosen human penmen.

If that claim is true, then the Bible is different from all other literature. It is not merely human and natural; it is *super*-human and *super*natural. Its inspiration is a miracle. Its revealing how the universe began, and how the pre-Adamite earth was refashioned to become the abode of mankind, is a miracle. Its foretelling of events and details accurately, centuries in advance, even to the end of time, and even beyond time, is a miracle.

Moreover, the Bible *records* miracles — scores of them — such as the dividing of the sea to let the hundreds of thousands of Israelites cross over, the falling of fire from heaven on Mount Carmel at the prayer of Elijah, the bodily resurrection of the Lord Jesus Christ.

There is a certain kind of biblical scholarship today which

thinks it must be all the time apologizing to modern science for the supernatural in the Bible. It has tried in one way or another to explain away all the biblical miracles; but if we are honestly to accept the clear wording of the Scripture records, then as plainly as can be, the Bible means us to understand that they were *miracles.*

We evangelicals take the position that if the *evidences* are demonstrably sound for the inspiration of the Bible and the veracity of its records, then we accept them. The Bible openly offers its credentials to human reason and logic. New Testament Christianity invites investigation and makes appeal to evidence. We believe that the truly scientific attitude is to weigh the evidence, and thereby reach a verdict.

Our intuitive sense of logical fairness is strangely jarred, therefore, when a seminary professor or some Christian minister says to us, "Your evidences mean nothing to me. If they were a hundred times stronger they would still be valueless. As a modern man in an age of science and in a universe of inviolable natural law, I reject all talk of 'miracle' as absolutely inadmissible."

We have to agree with such a man that our appeal to evidences is lost upon *him,* but we cannot help adding that in the name of science he is being utterly unscientific. To reject summarily all evidence for miracle on the *a priori* assumption that miracle is impossible, is to forget that the *a priori* assumption itself was first reached by weighing evidence. It is an even worse fault to let that *a priori* assumption shut out all further and more recent evidence.

Actually, the man who absolutely disallows the possibility of miracle is no longer "modern." The same attitude was manifesting itself a hundred-and-fifty years ago among Germany's radical theologians. Nobody has ever voiced it more strongly than David Strauss in his brilliant *Leben Jesu* (1835).

What is more, if I correctly interpret what I read, modern science itself is now much more inclined to accept the credibility of miracle. Some of the world's leading scientists are men of Christian faith who accept the Bible from cover to cover. They accept it as the Word of God on grounds of valid evidence. Is it not strange that when science is now much more open to evidence for miracle, a certain brand of Christian theologian still adamantly refuses it? Does it not show again that liberalism is not so much a matter of scholarship as an attitude of mind, a spirit, a temper, a set refusal to admit the supernatural in Christianity? Professing themselves to be modernly broad, the antisupernaturalists have become too narrow to admit even the soundest evidence if it is against them.

Well, we must leave them and feel sorry for them. The kind of study which we are here opening up can have little meaning for such as they. On the other hand, if we have "eyes to see and ears to hear," I believe that our present line of exposition will carry its own weight of edifying evidence to our minds, that the Bible is indeed the inspired Word of God. I entitle my theme:

THE BIBLE DOCTRINE OF THE LAMB

To my own mind, the most satisfying proofs that the Bible is divinely inspired are not those which one "reads up" in volumes of religious evidences or Christian apologetics, but those which we discover for ourselves in our own study of the Book.

To the prayerful explorer the Bible has its own way of revealing its internal credentials. One fascinating study-trail which continually repays exploration and always confirms faith in the divine origin of the Bible is that which we call "the progress of doctrine." Let me clearly explain what we mean by that term.

When we evangelicals speak about "progress of doctrine" in the Bible we do not mean, as certain others do, a groping progress from error to truth. To us, the whole Bible is the product of the Holy Spirit, but the revelation which it brings to us is progressive. By "progress of doctrine" we mean, so to speak, progress from the dimness of the dawn to the brightness of the noon. It is the same divine light which shines through all the pages, but the degree of the light increases as the revelation unfolds.

More particularly, by this "progress of doctrine" we mean that truths or teachings which first appear in Genesis or other early parts of the Scriptures are found to have a recurring mention and developing build-up right through the Bible, book after book, stage after stage, century after century, each successive mention contributing some further aspect in the progressive unfolding, until usually some New Testament passage is reached in which there is either a classic summary or a completive culmination. Indeed, in some instances, subjects which are first mentioned away back in early Genesis keep reappearing in succeeding books of Scripture until, in the closing pages of the New Testament, the Apocalypse unmistakably finalizes them.

In this "progress of doctrine" seldom does the first mention of a subject seem likely to be the first link in a concatenated series, nor do the human agents who figure in the series suspect that in what they say or do they are contributing to a developing divine revelation. That, however, only makes such progress of doctrine the more obviously supernatural and fascinating.

One outstanding instance of this progressive unfolding is the Bible doctrine of the Lamb; and it is that which we are to inspect somewhat in these studies. It is the kind of theme which, if we approach it with reverent and prayerful eagerness, will stir our hearts to love and prize and adore our Lord Jesus more than ever. I dare not claim originality for some of the germinative data, but the formulation and expansion of them are entirely our own. Let us then briefly examine the progressive doctrine of the Lamb. As an introduction, let me quote 1 Peter 1:18-21.

> Ye were redeemed, not with corruptible things, with silver or gold, from your vain manner of life handed down from your fathers; but with the precious blood of Christ, as of a lamb without blemish and without spot: who verily was foreordained before the foundation of the world, but was manifested in these last times for your sake, who through Him believe in God, who raised Him up from the dead, and gave Him glory, so that your faith and hope might be in God.

In the Bible there are *ten* notable passages in which the Lamb is conspicuously mentioned. They are as follows.

First, in Genesis 4 there is the account of *Abel* and his lamb.

Second, in Genesis 22 there is the incident in which *Abraham* offers the lamb in place of Isaac.

Third, in Exodus 12 there is the *Passover* lamb slain on the night before the exodus of the Israelites from Egypt.

Fourth, in the Book of Leviticus there is the *sin-offering* lamb which Israelites offered on the altar of sacrifice outside the tabernacle.

Fifth, in Isaiah 53 there is the *suffering* Lamb on whom "Jehovah laid the iniquity of us all."

Sixth, in the Gospel according to John, chapter 1, verses 29 to 36, there is the Lamb announced by *John the Baptist*: "Behold, the Lamb of God which beareth away the sin of the world."

Seventh, in Acts 8 there is the incident of the *Ethiopian official* traveling in his chariot on the Gaza road from Jerusalem, and reading about the Lamb in Isaiah 53, to whom Philip explains that the Lamb is Jesus the Messiah.

Eighth, in 1 Peter 1:18-21 there is the paragraph which we quoted by way of introduction, which tells us that we were redeemed with the precious blood of Christ, as of a *Lamb* "without blemish and without spot."

Ninth, in the Book of Revelation, chapter 5, there is the vision which dramatizes the enthronement of the Lamb in heaven.

Tenth, in Revelation 21 and 22 there is the final vision of the Apocalypse, in which the Lamb is seen reigning in the New Jerusalem, amid the "new heaven and new earth."

Successive Emphases

Those, then, are the ten special Lamb passages. Let us now look through them and observe the distinctive *emphases* developing successively through them. First, in Genesis 4:3-7a there is the account of Abel and his lamb:

> And in process of time it came to pass that Cain brought of the fruit of the ground an offering unto Jehovah. And Abel, he also brought of the firstlings of his flock and of the fat thereof. And Jehovah had respect unto Abel and to his offering; but unto Cain and to his offering He had not respect. And Cain was very wroth, and his countenance fell. But Jehovah said unto Cain, Why art thou wroth? and why is thy countenance fallen? If thou doest well, shalt

thou not be accepted? and if thou doest not well,
sin [or, perhaps more correctly, a sin-*offering*]
croucheth at the [tent] door.

We notice at once that in this Abel incident the emphasis is
upon the *necessity* of the Lamb. We are not told that the lamb
was slain, though presumably it was both killed and burned.
Cain's outwardly beautiful but bloodless offering was evidently
in disobedience to divine instruction. We know this from the
comment in Hebrews 11:5, that Abel offered his lamb "by
faith," that is, faith in what God had spoken about it. Cain's
offering had in it nothing of confessed sin or of need for propitiation. But God gave him another chance: "If thou doest
well [that is, according to what is required of thee] shalt thou
not be accepted? And if thou doest not well, a sin-offering
croucheth at the door." It is noteworthy that in the Hebrew
language the same word means both "sin" and "sin-*offering*,"
remarkably indicating the identification of the sinner with the
sin-offering.

Cain still disobeyed and was rejected. Thus, both through
Abel and through Cain, we see the indispensable necessity of
the Lamb.

Genesis 22

The second passage where the Lamb significantly figures is
the twenty-second chapter of Genesis, in the story of Abraham
and the lamb which he offered in place of Isaac. It will be
enough if we quote verses 6 to 8.

> And Abraham took the wood of the burnt of-
> fering, and laid it upon Isaac his son; and he
> took in his hand the fire and the knife; and they
> went both of them together. And Isaac spake
> unto Abraham his father, and said: . . . Behold
> the fire and the wood: but where is the lamb
> for a burnt offering? And Abraham said: My
> son, God will provide himself a lamb for a burnt
> offering. . . .

In this incident the emphasis is not upon the necessity of the
lamb, but upon God's *provision* of it: "God will provide himself the lamb." This is doubly emphasized by the way the incident ends. Just as the agonized patriarch lifts the knife, the
voice from heaven arrests him with these words: "Lay not
thine hand upon the lad. . . ." And in that moment Abraham
sees a ram caught in a thicket, which he at once understands is
to be offered instead of Isaac. God had indeed *provided* the
lamb. So impressed was Abraham that he named the place
Jehovah-jireh, which means "Jehovah will *provide*." Yes, that
is the aspect which is underscored — the *provision* of the Lamb.

Exodus 12

Here in this third passage we have the Passover lamb on the
night before the exodus of the Israelites from Egypt. And now
the emphasis is upon the *slaying* of the Lamb.

> Speak ye unto all the congregation of Israel, say-
> ing, In the tenth day of this month they shall

take to them every man a lamb, according to
their fathers' houses, a lamb for a household. . . .
And ye shall keep it up until the fourteenth day
of the same month, and the whole assembly of
the congregation shall kill it in the evening. And
they shall take of the blood, and strike it on the
two side posts and on the lintel of the houses
wherein they shall eat it. . . . Ye shall take a
bunch of hyssop, and dip it in the blood that is in
the basin, and strike the lintel and the two side
posts with the blood that is in the basin; and none
of you shall go out of the door of his house until
the morning. For Jehovah will pass through to
smite the Egyptians: and when he seeth the
blood upon the lintel and on the two side posts,
Jehovah will pass over the door, and will not
suffer the destroyer to come in unto your houses
to smite you.

vv. 3, 6, 7, 22, 23

So there had to be one lamb for each family, and it had to be
a male of the first year, without blemish (5). It was to be a
covering from the stroke of the destroying angel. Most em-
phatically of all, it must be *slain,* and its blood sprinkled pro-
tectively on the Hebrew dwellings. However blemishless, however qualified in itself the little lamb might be, it was of no
covering efficacy while still alive. Jehovah's word was, "When
I see the *blood,* I will pass over you" (13). Let it be duly
weighed: in Exodus 12, in the case of the paschal lamb, the
emphasis is on the *slaying* of the lamb.

Leviticus 16

And now, in the fourth place, we have the Lamb as set forth in the Book of Leviticus. That third book of the Pentateuch is a manual for Israel's priests, giving them instructions about the sacrifices which were to be offered, and informing them of regulations covering various other matters. All the way through Leviticus the emphasis is upon the *character* of the lamb. Some twenty times we are told that the Lord's offering must be "without blemish." Or, in the words of 22:21, "It shall be *perfect* to be accepted."

Isaiah 53

Now turn to Isaiah 53 for the fifth of these Lamb passages. Here we have what is perhaps the most famous and treasured of all the Isaian prophecies. The whole chapter is so well known that we need quote only verses 6 to 8:

> All we like sheep have gone astray; we have turned every one to his own way: and Jehovah hath laid on him the iniquity of us all.

> He was oppressed, and he was afflicted, yet he opened not his mouth. He is brought *as a lamb* to the slaughter, and *as a sheep* before its shearers is dumb, so he openeth not his mouth.

> By oppression and judgment he was taken away;

and who considers his generation? For he was cut off out of the land of the living: for the transgression of my people [saith Jehovah] he was stricken.

Here we take a big step forward in the developing revelation of the Lamb. Up to this point the lamb has been an animal, but now for the first time we learn that the Lamb God provides is a *Person*. *"He* was wounded for our transgressions." "Jehovah hath laid on *him* the iniquity of us all." *"He* is brought *as a lamb* to the slaughter." Yes, the Lamb is a *Person*.

John 1

In the sixth place we come to the first chapter of John's Gospel. From verse 19 onward we are at Bethabara (more correctly, Bethany) on the eastern side of the river Jordan, and away up in the direction of Galilee. We are among the crowds who attended John the Baptist's startling ministry, to hear his preaching that the long-awaited kingdom of heaven was at hand.

On one of those days a deputation from the Pharisees in Jerusalem came to interview John. Since the ascetic prophet was teaching that the leaders and people of Israel needed some peculiar cleansing and baptismal admission into a fellowship holier than that which came by membership in the elect nation, the Jewish leaders wanted to know what it was all about. John plainly told them, "I am not the Christ." But he added, "There standeth One among you whom ye know not: *he* it is [i.e. the Christ] who cometh after me." So John already knew Jesus, and who he really was. He had learned it when Jesus came for baptism in Jordan some days earlier. The "next day" after answering the deputation from Jerusalem, John sees Jesus coming to him and cries:

> "Behold, the *Lamb of God,* that taketh away the sin of the world!" (29).

So here the Lamb is not only a person; he is identified as *that* Person, even Jesus. By way of emphasizing this, verse 35 adds, "Again on the morrow John was standing, and two of his disciples; and looking upon Jesus as he walked John saith, Behold the Lamb of God!" So now we know *who* is the typified Lamb.

Acts 8

And now we move on to the eighth chapter of the Acts, where we have the seventh link in this tenfold chain of special reference to the Lamb. See the episode beginning at verse 26.

The angel of the Lord directs Philip the evangelist to the road from Jerusalem to Gaza. On that road, traveling southward in his chariot, is an important Ethiopian dignitary, chancellor of the exchequer to Candace, queen of the Ethiopians. As he sits in his chariot he is reading Isaiah 53. Philip calls, "Understandest thou what thou readest?" and the surprised official replies, "How can I, except someone shall guide me?" Then Philip joins him, and finds him reading, "He was led as a sheep to the slaughter, and as a lamb before his shearer is dumb, so he openeth not his mouth."

The narrative goes on to tell us that Philip "began at the same Scripture and preached unto him *Jesus.*" The result was that the Ethiopian requested baptism, and Philip said, "If thou believest with all thine heart, thou mayest." The Ethiopian replied, "I believe that Jesus Christ is the Son of God."[1]

The point here is that the Lamb of God is not only identified personally as Jesus, but that Jesus the Lamb is further identified as the promised *Christ,* the Son of God.

First Peter 1:18-21

From that, we pass now to the eighth of these ten passages on the Lamb. It is the passage we quoted at the outset.

> Ye were redeemed, not with corruptible things,
> with silver or gold, from your vain manner of life
> handed down from your fathers; but with pre-
> cious blood, as of a *lamb without blemish and
> without spot,* even the blood of Christ: who verily
> was foreordained before the foundation of the
> world, but was manifested at the end of the times

---

[1]To my own mind, it is a minor tragedy that verse 37 is omitted, except by marginal acknowledgment, in ERV, the ASV, and again in RSV. Our earliest New Testament manuscripts go back only as far as the fifth century, whereas Irenaeus, in his third book against *Heresies,* written as early as between A.D. 180 and 188, distinctly quotes that part of verse 37 which says, "I believe Jesus Christ to be the Son of God." And Cyprian (A.D. 200-258), in his third book of *Testimonies,* quotes the other part of the verse. So, long before the oldest existing manuscripts, verse 37 *must* have been in the codices of both the Greek and Latin churches.

for your sake, who through him believe in God,
who raised him up from the dead, and gave him
glory; so that your faith and hope might be in
God.

This passage is of pivotal importance in the developing doctrine of the Lamb. It looks both backward and forward. That
is, it gathers up all that has preceded it, and then adds a
startling new truth which points us on to wonderful consumma-
tions in the future.

Observe first how Peter's paragraph sums up all the different
aspects of the Lamb which we have encountered thus far. We
started with Abel, and saw the *necessity* of the Lamb. Here
it is in First Peter: "Not with corruptible things, with silver or
gold"; the indispensable *necessity* is the Lamb.

Then, in the Abraham-and-Isaac incident, we saw the *provision* of the Lamb. And here it is again in this paragraph from
First Peter; for the Lamb, Peter tells us, was *"foreordained* before the foundation of the world."

Next we saw the emphasis on the *slaying* of the Lamb in
the Passover drama, and here it appears again in this summary
by Peter. We are redeemed, not by the immaculate life or
sublime teaching of our Lord Jesus apart from his death, but by
the "precious *blood* of Christ."

Next, in Leviticus, we saw the repeated emphasis on the
character of the Lamb. It must be blemishless. So here in
First Peter our Lord is said to be a Lamb "without blemish and
without spot." It is that *character* of the Lamb which gives the
blood its atoning virtue.

In Isaiah 53 we found that Jehovah's Lamb is a *person.*
And in John 1 we saw that person identified as *Jesus.* In Acts 8
we saw Jesus the Lamb identified as the promised *Christ.* It is
all here in this paragraph from Peter's pen, for he tells us that
this fore-provided Lamb is the personal Lord Jesus Christ of the
Gospel.

Is there any special reason for this interim summary? There is. Having looked back over all those aspects of the Lamb which were already revealed, Peter's paragraph now includes the *resurrection* of the slain Lamb. "God . . . raised him up from the dead, and gave him glory."

This *resurrection* of the slain Lamb was something never fore-disclosed in Old Testament times. That the Lamb should *die* is foretold again and again; but nowhere is his resurrection predicted. With the light of the New Testament shining on the Old Testament, we who live in this gospel dispensation can now discern in certain parts of the Old Testament latent or typical anticipations of our Lord's resurrection, but nowhere was it clearly revealed, as were the other aspects of his saviorhood.

Observe also that as soon as Peter mentions the *resurrection* of the Lamb, he introduces the correlative feature of *hope*: "God raised him up . . . that your faith and *hope* might be in God." All the other aspects of the Lamb and his saving work call for "faith," but as soon as we see the *resurrection* of the slain Lamb, faith becomes crowned with wonderful new *hope*. So, what *is* this new hope? What of the Lamb and the future? We begin to see the answer to that question in the next great Lamb chapter, Revelation 5.

Revelation 5

In this further chapter we see the *enthronement* of the Lamb in heaven. It takes the whole chapter to describe it, but for the moment we need not quote more than verses 6 and 8.

And I saw in the midst of the throne and of the

> four living beings, and in the midst of the elders, a *Lamb* standing, as though it had been slain. . . . And the four living beings and the four and twenty elders fell down before the *Lamb,* having each one a harp, and golden bowls full of incense, which are the prayers of the saints.

So the Lamb is now in the throne of heaven, the very throne of the universe! What does *that* mean for the future? We find the answer in the tenth and last of these Lamb chapters, namely, Revelation 21 and 22.

Revelation 21-22

What a climax of never-ending glory is portrayed in these last two chapters of the New Testament! In a passage which seems to grow more wonderful every time we read it reflectively, we see the ultimate goal reached in the endless bliss of a sinless society here on this earth, with the curse and pain and tears and death all gone for ever. The untarnishable New Jerusalem forever supersedes the old. The earth itself is renewed and adapted to the new society. God himself dwells in the midst, and an ineffable, eternal day banishes darkness forever. It is indeed a sublime ending — an ending which merges into a prospect of *never*-ending felicity. The account runs from chapter 21:1 to 22:5, and reaches its climax in these words:

> And there shall be no curse any more; but the throne of God and of *the Lamb* shall be therein:

and his servants shall serve him; and they shall
see his face, and his name shall be on their foreheads. There shall be night no more. They
need no light of a lamp, neither light of the sun;
for the Lord God shall give them light; and they
shall reign unto the ages of the ages.

Thus, the final picture of the Lamb is that of his everlasting
kingship. He sits in the very throne of God — the "throne of
God and of the Lamb" — and reigns supreme in the glorious
queen city of God's new order upon this earth, away beyond
the Millennium, in those ages outlasting all time-measurement,
yet to unfold. His reign never ends. He is *King of Kings* for
ever!

Recapitulation

Those, then, are the ten great Lamb passages. Look back
over them now in recapitulation. (1) Genesis 4: Abel and his
lamb. (2) Genesis 22: Abraham and the Jehovah-Jireh lamb.
(3) Exodus 12: the Passover lamb. (4) Leviticus: the lamb
"without blemish." (5) Isaiah 53: the submissive and suffering lamb. (6) John 1: the Lamb recognized in human form.
(7) Acts 8: the Lamb and the Ethiopian chancellor. (8) the
Lamb in First Peter 1. (9) the Lamb in Revelation 5. (10)
the Lamb in the last two chapters of the Bible.

And what progress of emphasis, indeed, moves link by link
through these ten passages! (1) Abel: the *necessity* of the
Lamb. (2) Abraham: the *provision* of the Lamb. (3) the
Exodus: the *slaying* of the Lamb. (4) Leviticus: the *character*

of the Lamb. (5) Isaiah 53: the *personality* of the Lamb. (6) John 1: the *identifying* of the Lamb. (7) Acts 8: the *Christhood* of the Lamb. (8) First Peter 1: the *resurrection* of the Lamb. (9) Revelation 5: the *enthronement* of the Lamb in heaven. (10) Revelation 21 and 22: the *endless kingship* of the Lamb amid the "new heaven and new earth."

Progressive Doctrine

But now travel through those ten Lamb passages again, and see the remarkable progress of *doctrine* which they exhibit. In the case of Abel, we are simply told that the lamb was an "offering." The New Testament comment is that it was a "sacrifice" offered by "faith"; that is, it was a *propitiation* to a gracious but holy God who cannot tolerate sin. We need not read more into it than that, but neither can we read less. The lamb was a *propitiation.*

In the Abraham incident the emphasis is not upon propitiation, but upon *substitution,* for the lamb is offered as a substitute instead of Isaac.

Next, in the Passover story of Exodus 12, the emphasis is neither on propitiation nor on substitution, but on *protection.* The sprinkled blood on the door-frames is a protective covering from the angel of judgment and death.

In Leviticus, particularly in chapter 16 where we have the annual "Day of Atonement," the emphasis is upon complete *absolution* — absolution from guilt, in both its Godward and manward aspects.

That annual "Day of Atonement" wonderfully typified our Lord's atoning work on Calvary, and in order to show this the lamb had to be represented by two goats[2] — one "for Jehovah," as a sin-offering for the nation's guilt, and the other "for *azazel*" (or "removal," as the Hebrew word means).

Our King James Version translates that Hebrew word *azazel* as "scapegoat," but perhaps we are wiser to keep to the Hebrew word itself — *azazel,* that is, "removal." After the one goat had been slain as a sin-offering on behalf of the nation, Aaron the high priest was to lay both his hands on the head of the *azazel,* or "scapegoat," confessing over it "all the iniquities" of the nation, by which high priestly act all those sins were symbolically transferred to the *azazel* goat. Then the *azazel,* or goat of "removal," was driven away out to the wilderness, bearing upon itself (and thus "removing") all those sins, to be lost forever in the trackless wilderness, never to be remembered against Israel any more. See verses 7 to 10 with 21 and 22.

Thus, the goat offered as a sacrifice typified the Godward aspect of our Lord's atoning work for us, while the *azazel* goat typified the manward aspect, i.e., the removing of our guilt far from us forever. The two goats together therefore represent a complete and final *absolution.*

In Isaiah 53 all the foregoing aspects are included, but now the emphasis is on *expiation.* The suffering Lamb who is "wounded for *our* transgressions" expiates in his *own* soul and body the penalty of *our* sin.

In John 1, in the words, "Behold, the Lamb of God which beareth away the sin of the world," the emphasis is upon the complete *removal* of our sin, with all its ugly guilt and penalty. The Greek word means not only to bear, but to bear *away.*

taketh
in
KJV

[2]Let it be noted that in this one instance, and for a very meaningful reason, the two goats represent the one Lamb. Why were not two *lambs* chosen? The reason seems clear. Not in any detail must the typical ceremonies and offerings of the Mosaic ritual suggest that there is more than the one "Lamb of God which beareth away the sin of the world."

The immense, black barrier between God and our sinful race is *removed* in that one gigantic sin-bearing.

In Acts 8, where Philip preaches Jesus as the Lamb-Messiah-Savior to the high-ranking Ethiopian official, the emphasis is upon individual human *salvation* through the Lamb. On having the Lamb in Isaiah 53 explained to him, the Ethiopian exclaims, "I believe!" The end of the episode is: "And he went on his way rejoicing." What he had failed to find in Jerusalem, in the Law, in the Temple, in the ceremonials, he had found in Jesus Christ the Lamb — personal *salvation*.

In 1 Peter 1:18-21, the emphasis is upon *redemption* through the Lamb. "Ye were *redeemed* . . . with precious blood, as of a lamb without blemish and without spot, even the blood of Christ." This is redemption, not just as an objective concept, but as a received and possessed reality.

In Revelation 5 the emphasis is upon *government by the Lamb*. He is not only risen and ascended; he now sits in sovereign control over history and destiny, as "the Lamb in the midst of the throne"!

Finally, in Revelation 21 and 22 we see the transfigured saints reigning in *eternal glory* through the Lamb. "The throne of God and of the Lamb shall be therein . . . The Lord God shall illumine them, and they shall reign unto the ages of the ages." Yes, that is the final emphasis — *eternal glory* through the Lamb!

How wonderful is this developing biblical theology of the Lamb! See the ten focus-points in kaleidoscopic movement — (1) in Genesis 4, *propitiation* through the Lamb; (2) in Genesis 22, *substitution* by the Lamb; (3) in Exodus 12, *protection* through the Lamb; (4) in Leviticus, *absolution* through the Lamb; (5) in Isaiah 53, *expiation* by the Lamb; (6) in John 1, *sin-removal* by the Lamb; (7) in Acts 8, personal *salvation* through the Lamb; (8) in First Peter 1, *redemption* through the Lamb; (9) in Revelation 5, *government* by the

Lamb; (10) in Revelation 21—22, *eternal glory* through the Lamb!

Progressive Expansiveness

And now travel once more through those ten passages exhibiting the Lamb, and observe their progressive *expansion.*

In the case of Abel, we are told simply that the lamb was offered. It was offered as a propitiation for *sin.*

In the Abraham-and-Isaac incident the lamb was offered in the place of *one person,* namely, Isaac.

In the case of the Passover, each family must have its own lamb. It was the Lamb for *one family.*

In the book of Leviticus, in the typical ritual on the annual "Day of Atonement," we see the Lamb for *one nation.*

Next, in Isaiah's great picture of the suffering Lamb-Messiah we find: "He shall sprinkle many nations"[3] — which looks beyond Israel; also, in verse 8, "He shall make many righteous, for he shall bear their iniquities." Here we have the Lamb for *all the elect.*

In John 1: "Behold the Lamb of God which beareth away the sin of the world," we have the Lamb for *the whole world.*

In Acts 8 it is the Lamb for each individual — not for the Jew only, but also for that dark-skinned Gentile Ethiopian. It is the Lamb for *"whosoever."*

In First Peter 1 it is the Lamb "foreordained from before the foundation of the world" — that is, the Lamb for *all history.*

---

[3]On meaning of "sprinkling" here see Ellicott Commentary *in loco.*

In Revelation 5, where the Lamb is enthroned in heaven, we see the Lamb *for the universe*.

In Revelation 21 and 22, where he reigns in endless glory amid the new heaven and new earth, we see the Lamb *for all eternity*.

Think of it: (1) the Lamb for *sin;* (2) the Lamb for *one person;* (3) the Lamb for *one family;* (4) the Lamb for *one nation;* (5) the Lamb for all *the elect;* (6) the Lamb for *the world;* (7) the Lamb for *"whosoever";* (8) the Lamb for *all history;* (9) the Lamb for the whole *universe;* (10) the Lamb for *all eternity!*

Supernatural Inspiration

Is all this progressive presentation of the Lamb a product of blind chance or fortuitous coincidence? According to some moderns, I may be old-fashioned and naive, but to me this Bible doctrine of the Lamb is another internal evidence of supernatural inspiration. It confirms to me that the whole Bible is a developing unfolding of divine revelation, and that the whole of it is the written Word of God. If that is being old-fashioned, then let me stay old-fashioned, for I believe that this good old fashion will still be new and true when the new fashion of the present hour has become dead and buried, with few mourners at the funeral. I recommend to one and all: Let such biblical phenomena as this progressive doctrine of the Lamb be a reassurance that these sixty-six documents which comprise our Bible are the "living oracles" of the Almighty.

Divine Testimony

To that I would add: Let this Bible doctrine of the Lamb show us what *God* thinks about the Lamb. In one way or another, right through the Bible, it is Jesus as the *Lamb* who has the preëminence. All other disclosures, whether through Pentateuchal law or Israelitish history, whether psalmodic or philosophic, whether prophetic or doctrinal, whether visional or didactic, all are subservient to this onward-moving unveiling of truth concerning the *Lamb*. Supremely, our Bible is God's testimony to the *Lamb*. Should not our own testimony be in line with God's? Should not the *Lamb* be the outshining center and dominating accent of all our Christian preaching and witness-bearing?

Tenfold Message

Think back again over the tenfold progress: the necessity of the Lamb, the divine provision of the Lamb, the slaying of the Lamb — right on to the heavenly enthronement and eternal sovereignty of the Lamb. Are not all these needing new enunciation in the pulpit ministry and public evangelism of today?

Glance back over some of those ten *doctrinal* emphases of the Lamb: propitiation, substitution, absolution, expiation, redemption. All these, and indeed all ten, are being denied, or glossed away, or disdained today by ecclesiastical scholars at the one extreme, and in the hazy sophisms of crude "hippies" at the other extreme. One of our easiest dangers just now is to give way, either to the pressures of humanistic theologians, or to the loud rebellions of misguided young collegians.

Already we are seeing everywhere around us today the sorry repercussions of the new and popular *false* gospels. You have only to turn on your television or scan your newspaper to see that the part of American society which gets most publicity at present is wallowing in muck and mire. Instead of accommodating our message to changing theological predilections or to carnalized social standards, we should preach with more consecrated resolve than ever our central, glorious gospel of the *Lamb* — the Lamb of Calvary, of resurrection victory, of all transcendent enthronement; the one and only true Savior, and the predestined Administrator of a soon-coming new age!

See that stately oak tree, proudly reigning on yonder hillside. How did it become the noble, mighty giant that it now is? Was it by bowing and cringing to hostile winds or sudden tempests? No, it was by holding on and standing firm. The more the storms tore in among the branches and ripped off the leaves, the deeper went the roots, and the stronger grew the trunk, and the sturdier became the branches. Even so, this is no time for us to be apologizing for our evangelical message. Like Goliath's sword, there is "none like it"! I believe that if we hold our ground, and refuse to pander to the whims of a sick society, and preach more prayerfully than ever *redemption through the Lamb,* we shall yet win new triumphs.

As we remember again how we ourselves have become saved through the Lamb, let us exult yet more gratefully that the "precious blood" shed on Calvary still cleanses from all sin and brings us eternal salvation. Let William Cowper's lines become afresh the language of our hearts:

> E'er since by faith I saw the stream
> Thy flowing wounds supply,
> Redeeming love has been my theme,
> And shall be till I die.

Then, in a nobler, sweeter song
    I'll sing Thy power to save,
With sinless heart and raptured tongue,
    In triumph o'er the grave.

CHAPTER TWO

THE CENTRALITY OF THE LAMB

Jesus is King!
True King of Israel, David's great Son,
Hope of the fathers, Heir to the throne;
Lion of Judah, Lamb that was slain,
True King of Israel yet shall He reign.

Jesus is King!
King of the angels, reigning in light,
King of His people, glorious in might,
Victor o'er Hades, Judge of all men,
King of all nations yet shall He reign.

Jesus is King!
King of all regions and ages of time,
King of the heaven of heavens sublime,
King of all creatures in every domain,
King of the universe yet shall He reign.

Jesus is King!
Sovereign of sovereigns, King evermore,
Godhead Incarnate, all must adore,
Soon now returning to end war and pain,
Boundless in empire yet shall He reign.
Jesus is King!

—J. S. B.

OUR LORD JESUS is both the center and the circumference of divine revelation. As the sun is the center of our solar system, and also the power which holds it together, so Christ is the magnetic center of Scripture, and the unifying theme which makes all the three-score-and-six books of the Bible one self-consistent whole.

As Christ is the central *figure* of biblical revelation, so the Cross is the central *factor*. Whatever else our Bible may or may not be, it is distinctively and preëminently the book of *salvation from sin,* and its many-sided doctrine of salvation both centers in and radiates from the Christ of the *Cross*. The "precious blood" of Calvary, so to speak, sprinkles every page. The doctrine of redemption by the *Lamb* runs through Holy Writ like a crimson cord holding all the various parts of the sacred canon together in one. Amid the present-day whirl of new ideas, let this shine all the more clearly in our thinking: Jesus, as the *Lamb of God,* is the center-point of that message which we are to preach.

In the preceding study, we reviewed the progressive *unfolding* of biblical disclosure concerning the Lamb, in ten notable passages. From those ten we now pick out *three;* and we may truly call them three classic passages exhibiting the *centrality* of the Lamb.

The three passages are: (1) Isaiah 53, (2) Revelation 5,

and (3) Revelation 21 and 22. Those three sections display the centrality of the Lamb in the following way.

1. The Lamb amid the throes of his agony — Isaiah 53.

2. The Lamb amid the throne of his glory — Revelation 5.

3. The Lamb amid the throng of his people — Revelation 21-22.

In Isaiah 53 we see the Lamb transfixed to the Cross here on earth. In Revelation 5 we see the Lamb triumphant on the throne in heaven. In Revelation 21 and 22 we see the Lamb transcendent forever in the "new heaven and new earth."

In the first of those three passages we look back to a humiliation which is now past. In the second we look up to an exaltation which is now present. In the third we look on to a consummation which is yet future.

THE CENTRALITY OF THE LAMB
IN BEARING OUR SIN

We turn first to Isaiah 53, where we see the centrality of the Lamb in the bearing of our sin. That chapter is the most famous of all Isaiah's prophecies. It is quoted or alluded to again and again in the New Testament, and invariably it is applied to our Lord Jesus. Indeed, Angus's *Bible Handbook* says, "This chapter is almost reproduced in the New Testament, and is applied at every point to Christ."

If we were to insist on strict chapter divisions, I suppose the fifty-third chapter should begin three verses earlier than it does, that is, at verse 13 of the preceding chapter. However, although those three verses introduce the new section, the "report" itself on our Lord's agonizing humiliation and ultimate exaltation does not begin until the first verse of the fifty-third chapter, in the words, "Who hath believed our *report?*"

In both a literary and a prophetic sense it is a wonderful chapter. It gathers into vivid concentration all the various scattered references of the Hebrew prophets to our Lord's redemptive work. In its photographic description of our Lord's unattractiveness and rejectedness, his unretaliating submissiveness and vicarious sufferings, his fearful travail and final triumph, it is a *tout ensemble* of sublime character unexcelled anywhere, either inside or outside the Bible.

Unfortunately, in our Authorized Version and in the English Revised, and in the American Standard Version, Isaiah 53 reads as prose, whereas in the original it is superb poetry, as more recent English versions show. It is not poetry in the mold of rhyme or rhythm, but the flexible Hebrew poetry of thought-parallelism. In Hebrew poetry there are three kinds of parallels: (1) completive, (2) contrastive, (3) constructive. Isaiah 53 consists of twenty-four *completive* parallels. Completive parallels are those in which the second member of a pair extends or completes the thought in the first member. For instance, the first completive parallel is,

> Who has believed our report?
> And to whom is Jehovah's arm revealed?

In line one the report is not received. In line two the Lord's arm is not revealed. Line one gives a human aspect. Line two gives a divine aspect. Line two grows out of line one: it expresses something on the Godward side which grows out of unbelief on the manward side in line one. In all such completive parallels that is the feature: the second member carries forward, or intensifies, or amplifies, or completes the content of the first member. Take just the next two parallels in this fifty-third chapter:

> For he grows up as a sapling before him,
> And like a root out of arid ground.

> He has no form or regality that we should regard
> him
> Or appearance that we should desire him.

We will not linger over these couplets or the others throughout the chapter, though there is a peculiar fascination about them. The one thing to which we here call attention as being noteworthy is, that the *exact center* of these twenty-four parallels is,

> *He is led as a lamb to the slaughter;*
> *As a sheep, dumb before its shearers.*

If we are to be truly modern, then of course our immediate reaction is to regard this as purely accidental: we are too "enlightened" to allow that divine inspiration would descend to mere grammatical contrivances (even though it *does* use alphabetic mnemonics in Lamentations and certain of the Psalms!). But if that reference to the Lamb at exact center-point is mere coincidence, is it not even more remarkable that in the verses *preceding* it there are just seven expressions of vicarious atonement viewed from the *human* side, while in the verses *following* it there are another seven expressions of vicarious atonement viewed from the *divine* side? Let me point them out. First, in the earlier half of the chapter: —

1. *"He* hath borne *our* griefs" (verse 4)

 2. "And carried *our* sorrows" (4)

3. *"He* was wounded for *our* trangressions" (5)

4. *"He* was bruised for *our* iniquities" (5)

5. "The chastisement of *our* peace is on *him"* (5)

6. "And with *his* stripes *we* are healed" (5)

7. "Jehovah hath laid on *him* the iniquity of us all" (6).

Notice, it is *"our* griefs" and *"our* sorrows"; *"our* transgressions" and *"our* iniquities." All seven are from *"our"* side, the human side of the Cross.

Each of these seven statements expresses one distinct aspect of our Lord's representative and substitutionary identification with us, until the final, comprehensive statement is reached: *"Jehovah* hath laid on him the iniquity *of us all"* — which makes our Lord's death on our behalf an *act of God,* not just a deed of men; i.e. an *atonement,* not just a crucifixion.

And now glance through the second half of the chapter. Here we find seven expressions of vicarious atonement viewed from the *divine* side. Some of them are so worded that we hear God speaking through the pronoun "my"; or else, instead of "our," we now have *"their,"* as though God is viewing the Cross objectively.

1. "For the transgression of *my* people *he* was stricken" (8)

2. *"Thou* shalt make his soul an offering for sin" (10)

3. "By his knowledge shall *my* righteous Servant justify many" (11)

Not our but their

4. "For he shall bear *their* iniquities" (11)

5. "He was numbered with the transgressors" (12)

6. "And he bore the sin of many" (12)

7. "And made intercession for the transgressors" (12).

Well, there it is: seven aspects of vicarious atonement from *our* point of view, then seven aspects of it from *God's* side; and between the two sevens,

> *He is led as a lamb to the slaughter;*
> *As a sheep, dumb before its shearers.*

Are we still quite sure that its center-position happened accidentally? That is where it *belongs*. That is where the prophet-poet *put* it, speaking in the Holy Spirit. That is where *God* has put the Lamb — absolutely *central* in our redemption and salvation.

In this fifty-third chapter of Isaiah, this prophetic Passion-poem describing our Savior's vicarious sufferings, every strophe, every couplet, should be examined and pondered separately. We are dealing with supernatural literature in which every word is carefully placed and full of meaning. Let me here touch on just two of the poetic parallels. The first of those which actually declare the *vicarious* nature of our Lord's sufferings says,

> Surely it was our griefs he bore;
> It was our sorrows he carried.

Note the two verbs here: He *"bore"* and he *"carried."* Neither of them means to bear *away*. Thank God, our Lord *did* bear our guilt away from us for ever, but that is not the emphasis here. Both the Hebrew verbs used here stress the idea of his bearing our sins and sorrows as a consciously endured pressure of *weight*.

We need only reflect on what the fearful pressure of our whole race's sin, guilt, and sorrow must have been on the mind of our Lord to find ourselves soon lost in wondering thought too deep for words.

Even during the three years of his public ministry that burden must have pressed heavily upon him. In some mysterious way even then he became inwardly identified with the very sicknesses which his miracles healed, for Matthew 8:17 tells us that in those healings he fulfilled "that which was spoken by Isaiah the prophet: himself took our infirmities, and bare our sicknesses." He suffered even as he healed.

But it was as he drew near to Gethsemane, with its agony and sweat of blood, that the pressure intensified into a monstrous, crushing horror. Mark 14:33 tells us that he "began to be sore amazed and very heavy." The Greek verb translated as "sore amazed" is an awesome word to be used of our divine Savior. It means to be astounded, staggered, bewildered, utterly dumbfounded. The root meaning of the second verb is "not at home" — as though our Lord was driven beyond himself in an "anguish of the soul struggling to free itself from the body under such pressure of mental distress."

That we are not overstating the force of those two verbs may be seen in the way recent Greek scholars translate them. To mention only two: Weymouth renders the phrase, "full of terror and distress," and Moffatt gives it as "appalled and agitated."

> Oh, never, never can we know
> That crushing weight of sin and woe,

When He, our great Sinbearer bled,
The Lamb of Calvary, in our stead.

But take just one more couplet from Isaiah 53. It is in that fifth verse, and is unspeakably precious to all those of us who have fixed our hope of eternal salvation on that Lamb of Calvary.

He is wounded for our transgressions,
And is bruised for our iniquities.

That word "wounded" represents a Hebrew verb which more strictly means "pierced." After looking up its use in other parts of the Old Testament I think there is reason to translate it as "pierced" here. It points to the spear which was driven into our Lord's side, to the iron spikes which transfixed him to the rough beam and transom, and to the crown of piercing thorns which tore his brow.

That other verb in the couplet — "bruised" — is a fearful word to be used in such a connection. It means to crush or beat to pieces! It does not refer so much to our Lord's outward, physical sufferings as to the inconceivable extreme of his inward excrucuation.

The prophet sees it all in the present tense — "He is pierced . . . he is bruised," and that is how we should see it again in times of prayerful contemplation. It is true that we should always see the Cross in the light of our Lord's resurrection. It is true that he is no longer on that Cross. Yet equally truly there is a sense in which our Lord and that Cross are united forever. As we see him rising from the dead and ascending to heaven, our exulting gratitude ascends to God with him; nevertheless, if we want the deepest love of our hearts to well up and overflow toward him, we must keep seeing, in vivid memory and adoring contemplation, those pierced hands and

God help me to do this!

feet, that spear-torn side, that thorn-crowned brow, that Cross of sin-atoning anguish.

Most of us, in these days of rush and speed, spend far too little time in rapt contemplation of that Cross. We are needing to relearn the need and enrichment of lingering there. We preachers need to spend hours of aloneness before that Cross, with our Bible open at Isaiah 53, slowly going over it, line by line. If we are really to preach the Cross of Christ with compelling influence, we need inwardly to *see* it, as Isaiah did, with a vividness which breaks and melts and disturbs and inspires us. Every sermon on the Cross should come to our hearers wet with the preacher's tears.

Years ago I knew a fine Christian man in Canada. He was born and bred among the poor. At an early age he had to leave school and go to work. While still young he came to know the Lord Jesus as his Savior. He started a small business, and covenanted to give one-tenth of all his earnings to God. His business grew and grew until it was one of the largest of its kind in Canada. Faithfully he gave his tithe to the Lord. Then he made it a fifth, then a quarter, then a half, then three-quarters, then nine-tenths, until eventually he was running the whole business practically to make money for supporting the Lord's work in various ways. Thousands received financial help from him without ever knowing where it came from.

One day I asked him what brought about his conversion to Christ. He replied, "It was the example of my godly father." Then he told me he was one of four boys who grew up in the little old home. From their youngest days their father used to gather them round his knee, while he read to them from the Bible and then prayed with them. On Sunday evenings he always read Isaiah 53. With a glow on his face he would start to read it. Then, on reaching verse 4, "Surely he hath borne our griefs," or verse 5, "He was wounded for our transgressions; he was bruised for our iniquities," his voice would falter, his throat would become husky, the tears would begin to drip down his cheeks, and he would have to say in broken syllables, "I'm sorry, boys, I canna' go on; it's too upsettin' — that such a dear, divine Savior should suffer for us sinners . . . like *that!*"

My friend added, "Sometimes my dad would struggle on a bit, but I never once knew him to get right through Isaiah 53. Even if he managed to get beyond verses 5 and 6, he never got beyond verse 7 — 'He is led *as a lamb to the slaughter.*' It broke him down to think that the Son of God should suffer for us 'like that.' "

In the deepest sense of the words, can we *ever* get beyond that seventh verse? *He,* the Creator of stars and systems and aeons, the Firstborn of all creation, in whom all things cohere, the delight of the Father's bosom, *"He* is led as a *lamb* to the *slaughter"!* Can any Christian heart ever get over that as long as eternity lasts? Those nail-torn hands and feet are more marvelous to us than twice ten-billion stars. Those Calvary scars shine with lovelier luster than all the flashing gems of the New Jerusalem.

As we bring the eye of a telescope or the lens of a camera into clear focus upon an object, so the fifty-third chapter of Isaiah sets the *Lamb* in clear focus as the *center-point.* There it is, between those two sevens which express vicarious atonement, first from the human side, and then from the divine — which is only another way of saying that the *Holy Spirit* has put the Lamb there. There is no soul-saving message for sinners apart from the Lamb. No man is truly preaching the gospel who leaves out the Lamb or makes him anything other than the vital center.

In these days much so-called Christian scholarship and preaching sneers with fancied intellectual superiority at the idea of salvation through "the blood." Much that goes under the name of Christianity among our Protestant denominations is a new version of the *Cain* religion which wants to worship God with bouquets of flowers and fruits but refuses the sacrificial Lamb of propitiation and atonement. There is a humanistic elegance about it, but it has no confession that the members of Adam's fallen race are hell-deserving sinners needing redemption and regeneration. God rejects it. What is more, it leaves sinful man fundamentally unchanged. Cain would not lower himself to shed the blood of a poor little lamb; it was so "cruel"; yet he *would* in anger shed the blood of his own brother! If you want to know what religion without the Lamb does, look around at the pitiful wreck of morals and decency in Christendom today!

Let there be no apology in our preaching of the Lamb. Instead of secretly wondering whether we are preaching something outmoded or no longer relevant, let the desperate breakdown today be a new call to uplift the Lamb more than ever as *the vital center* of the only gospel which truly saves men!

THE CENTRALITY OF THE LAMB
IN WEARING THE CROWN

We turn now to the Book of Revelation, to the other two passages where the centrality of the Lamb is especially displayed. The first of the two is chapter 5, where we see the Lamb enthroned as *universal Administrator.*

The setting of this chapter is one of surpassing magnificence. In all of Holy Writ there is nothing to eclipse the grandeur and majesty of the scene which is here unveiled to us. The vision is of the rainbow-circled, glory-flashing throne of the Deity in the heaven of heavens, with the heavenly worshipers prostrating themselves around the throne in profound adoration and exulting praise. The vision quickly moves on to the climactic act in which the slain but now risen Lamb is constituted Joint-Occupant with the eternal Father in the seat of supreme authority. Thereupon the chapter reaches its spectacular and moving finale with the "one hundred millions" and "millions" more of angels, and all other beings throughout the universe, unitedly expressing themselves in a thunder of adoring praise to the Lamb-Lion-King amid the throne! Look at verses 1 to 5.

> And I saw in the right hand of him that sat on the throne a book written within and on the back, sealed with seven seals. And I saw a strong angel proclaiming with a loud voice: Who is worthy to open the book, and to loose the seals thereof? And no one in heaven or on the earth or under the earth was able to open the book or to look thereon.
>
> And I wept much because no one was found worthy to open the book or to look thereon. And one of the elders saith unto me: Weep not; behold, the Lion of the tribe of Judah, the Root of David, hath overcome to open the book and the seven seals thereof.

That seven-sealed book or scroll obviously is not the book of the past, for that is already unrolled and open. Nor is it the record of the unfolding present, for the hand of time itself is unrolling that. It is the book of the *yet-to-be,* revealing the finalities of human history, the winding up of present mysteries, the future climaxes of the divine purpose, and the ultimate issues of human destiny. We know that such is the meaning of the seven-sealed book because of what we see and hear and learn as the Lamb afterwards successively opens the seven seals.

It is not surprising that John "wept much" because no one

was found equal to breaking the seven seals, for is there anything of more concern to us human beings than to learn the ultimate outcome of the mysterious conflict of good and evil through the ages — and to know what our destiny will be in that endless future on the other side of the grave? We recall the consternation of Egypt's magicians when none of them could unseal the meaning of Pharaoh's dream — and how Joseph "overcame" to "unloose" the meaning of it, for doing which he was exalted by Pharaoh to be "over all the land of Egypt." We remember, too, the furious threat of Nebuchadnezzar to "destroy all the wise men of Babylon" because they could not interpret his forgotten dream — and how Daniel unlocked the mystery and meaning of it, for which he was exalted to be "ruler over the whole province of Babylon." There was the same kind of scene when the awesome handwriting appeared on the palace wall at Belshazzar's feast, and only Daniel could unseal its fateful message.

On an immeasurably grander scale, such is the vision in Revelation 5. Those seven seals symbolize not only the sacred inviolability of the scroll, but also the sevenfold completeness of the revelation contained in it. Only one hand in the universe can unfasten those seals, for there is only the One who is "worthy" to do so.

But why must he be *"worthy"?* It is because the unsealing of that book carries with it *the administrative authority to dispense its contents* — just as, in a much lesser sense, the unsealing of the royal dreams lifted Joseph and Daniel to the highest administrative authority. In other words, the One who can unloose those seals belongs in that rainbow-circled throne as the Executive of the Godhead. That is why, coinciding with our Lord's taking the book, John suddenly sees the Lamb "in the midst of the throne."

The first big wonder which we should clearly appreciate is that this chapter describes not something which is yet to happen but something which has occurred *already.* Admittedly, there are prospects in it which will reach their final fulfilment in the yet-future, but the main event, i.e. the enthronement of the Lamb, has happened already. Our Lord is even *now* in that Throne of thrones. We know this from a verb which occurs in verse 5: "The Lion of the tribe of Judah hath *overcome* to open the book." In the Greek the verb tense is the aorist, which is more exactly rendered here as *overcame*. It links back at once to chapter 3:21, where our risen Lord says, "To him that overcometh will I grant to sit with me in my throne (i.e. his messianic throne), even as I also *overcame* and sat down (note the past tense again) with my Father in *his* throne." So our ascended Lord himself tells us that when he sent those letters to the seven churches his investiture as supreme Administrator "in the midst of the Throne" had already taken place.

What a comfort it is, in these days of widespread moral breakdown, of defiant lawlessness, and social violence, and unblushing sexualism, and organized anti-Godism, and overhanging threat of nuclear war — what a comfort to know that despite all appearances to the contrary, the sovereign control of history and destiny is *still* in the hands which bear the nail-prints, and that these divinely permitted latter-day excesses are the very things which (as foretold) will precipitate his return in flaming power to trample out all such evil and bring in his global Christocracy!

But now glance at a few of the arresting features of this fifth chapter. The elder says to John, "Weep not; the Lion of the tribe of Judah, the Root of David, overcame to open the book." John therefore looks to see the Lion, but instead, to his utter surprise, he sees a *Lamb* right in the midst of all that glory — a Lamb with all the marks of having just been killed and yet "standing" there alive, as the center, along with God himself, of all that celestial splendor!

So the Lamb is the Lion! Here is the supreme vindication of the truth that right is might, that humility is majesty, that the final inheritance is with the meek, that light has the final victory over darkness, and that virtue shall at last trample evil underfoot. The Lamb who once was *slain* is the Lion who now must *reign*. The Victim is the Victor! The Crucified is the Crowned! The Servant and Savior of all is the Sovereign and Ruler of all. As Lamb he is Redeemer. As Lion he is King. He is the Lamb-Lion Redeemer-King.

Observe in verses 5 and 6 the seven great facts about the Lamb (like other symbolic sevens in Scripture, comprised of four and three) — four things which he *is,* and three attributes which he *has;* four features belonging to his *human* nature, and three pertaining to his *divine* being. Note first the four aspects of his humanity:

1. The "Lion of Judah," that is, the promised Deliverer of his people.

2. The "Root of David," that is, the promised Shepherd-King.

3. The "Lamb slain," that is, the promised Sin-bearer and Redeemer.

4. The "Worthy One," that is, the promised "glory of Israel," in whom is fulfilled all that seers ever saw and prophets ever promised and psalmists ever sang.

See now the three infinite attributes predicated of him. The Lamb has "seven horns, and seven eyes which are the seven spirits of God sent forth into all the earth." The horn is the symbol of *strength.* Seven is, among other significations, the number of completeness, of *perfection.* Thus we have here three infinite attributes:

1. "Seven horns," that is, perfect power — *omnipotence.*

2. "Seven eyes," that is, perfect wisdom —
omniscience.

3. "Seven spirits into all the earth" — *Omni-presence.*

Those are the attributes of God. The Lamb, besides being promised Deliverer, Governor, Redeemer, and Glory of Israel, is *God Incarnate!* He to whom these divine attributes are ascribed must not only be exalted, he must be *worshiped.* Therefore we are immediately told that "the four living beings, and four-and-twenty elders fell down before the *Lamb,* having, every one of them, harps, and golden vials full of odors which are the prayers of saints." The harps represent worship in the form of *praise.* The incense-vials represent worship in the form of *prayer.* The same kind of praise and prayer which are offered to God are now offered to the *Lamb,* that is, to the risen and exalted Lord Jesus as *God the Son incarnate in humanhood.* There is no unitarianism in heaven! Our Lord Jesus is no mere ideal man with a God-given laurel on his head; neither is he some exalted demiurge or demigod of the Jehovah's Witnesses brand. In that pure worship up yonder, where the Lamb is "in the midst of the Throne," he is worshiped not only as a "son of God," but as *God the Son.*

See now the tremendous climax of the whole scene. The countless myriads of angel hosts unite in the following sublime outburst of sevenfold praise to the Lamb: "Worthy is the Lamb that was slain, to receive: (1) the power, (2) the riches, (3) the wisdom, (4) the might, (5) the honor, (6) the glory, (7) the blessing"!

Then, augmenting and consummating the praise of the angelic hosts, the whole vast universe joins in the super-glorious anthem of acclamation described in the closing verses of the chapter. "And every creature which is in heaven, and on the earth, and under the earth, and on the sea, and all that are in them, I heard saying,

> 'Blessing, and honor, and glory, and dominion,
> unto him that sitteth on the throne, and to the
> *Lamb, unto the ages of the ages.'* "

How plain is the meaning of all this! God has put the Lamb in the place of absolute supremacy and centrality. Let us keep him where God has put him! He is central in prophecy and history, central in the worship of heaven, central in the adoration of saints and angels, central in the government and ultimate homage of the whole universe, central in his atonement as the one true Savior of men; central in his exaltation as the one true King of all creation.

THE CENTRALITY OF THE LAMB
IN SHARING HIS GLORY

Finally, look at the third passage where the centrality of the Lamb is outstandingly exhibited, Revelation 21 and 22. These last two chapters of the Apocalypse are the matchlessly sublime consummation of divine revelation as given to us in the Holy Scriptures. See again the opening words of chapter 21.

> And I saw a new heaven and a new earth: for
> the first heaven and the first earth are passed
> away; and the sea is no more. And I saw the

holy city, new Jerusalem, coming down out of
heaven from God, made ready as a bride
adorned for her husband.

So the passage which ensues is not a description of heaven,
but of a "city" which "comes down out of heaven" and is set
up here on this earth. In verse 24 we are told that "the *nations*
shall walk by the light of it; and the kings of the *earth* bring
their glory into it." Verse 26 adds that the "glory and honor
of the *nations*" shall be brought to it, and 22:2 tells us that
the tree of life made accessible again through it shall yield its
fruit monthly for the "healing [i.e. continually renewed health]
of the *nations*." See the glory of that apocalyptic city:

And he carried me away in the Spirit to a great
and high mountain, and showed me the holy
city, New Jerusalem, coming down out of heaven
from God, having the glory of God. Her light
was like unto a stone most precious, as it were a
jasper stone, clear as crystal. . . . And the
building of the wall thereof was jasper; and the
city was pure gold, like unto pure glass . . . And
the twelve gates were twelve pearls . . . (21:
10, 11, 18, 21).

Yet we miss the sublimest meaning unless we see that it is
the *Lamb* who is the center of it all. In the description of this
queen city amid the "new heaven and new earth," running
from 21:1 to 22:5, there are just *seven* references to the Lamb.
Well may we gratefully wonder at what they tell us.

1. "Come hither; I will show thee the bride, the
wife of the *Lamb*" (21:9). So the Lamb is the
Bridegroom.

2. "The city had twelve foundations, and in them the names of the twelve apostles of the *Lamb*" (21:14). So the Lamb is the *foundation*.

3. "I saw no temple . . . the Lord God Almighty and the *Lamb* are the temple" (21:22). So the Lamb is the *temple*.

4. "The glory of God did lighten it, and the *Lamb* is the light thereof" (21:23). So the Lamb is the luminary or *radiance*.

5. "Only they [enter] that are written in the book of life of the *Lamb*" (21:27). So the Lamb is the *portal*.

6. "A pure river of water of life, clear as crystal, from the throne of God and the Lamb" (22:1). So the Lamb is the *life*.

7. "The throne of God and of the Lamb shall be in it" (22:3). So the Lamb is the *King*.

Think of it — this sevenfold relationship of the Lamb to that ineffable city and society of the new world which is yet to be. The Lamb is the *Bridegroom*. The Lamb is the *foundation*. The Lamb is the *temple*. The Lamb is the *radiance*. The Lamb is the *portal*. The Lamb is the *life*. The Lamb is the *King* — the center of everything!

How sublimely wonderful is this sevenfold relationship between the heavenly Bridegroom and that queen city of the new earth! How rapturously it lights up the indissoluble bond that binds the people of Christ to their Lord and Savior! The Lamb is the Bridegroom and his people are the bride, so it is a *loving* union. The Lamb is the foundation and his people are the building, so it is a *lasting* union. The Lamb is both the temple and the object of his people's worship, so it is an *adoring* union.

The Lamb is the luminary or eradiating glory-light, so it is a *transfiguring* union. The Lamb is the portal and "nothing that defileth" can ever gain access, so it is a *holy* union. The Lamb is the life and we live in his life for ever, so it is a *life*-renewing union. The Lamb is the King and his people reign with him for ever, so it is a *royal* union.

Thus the Lamb is the ever-living, ever-loving, everlasting center and supreme glory of the celestial city and its sinless society. The light of the city is the *face* of Jesus. The music of the city is the *Name* of Jesus. The harmony of the city is the *praise* of Jesus. The theme of the city is the *love* of Jesus. The joy of the city is the *presence* of Jesus. The employment of the city is the *service* of Jesus. The strength of the city is the *omnipotence* of Jesus. The magnetic center and super-glory of the city is *Jesus himself*. The duration of the city is the *eternity* of Jesus.

> Jerusalem the golden,
>   With fadeless treasures blest,
> Oh, heavenly Zion glorious,
>   By raptured saints possessed!
> I know not, Oh, I know not
>   What joys await me there,
> What radiancy of glory,
>   What bliss beyond compare.

As we think of what "awaits us there," perhaps we can sympathetically enter into the wistful sentiment of the old Puritan who said, "When I get yonder, I'll spend the first thousand years gazing on Jesus; then I'll have a look around"!

> The Bride eyes not her raiment,
>   But her beloved's face;
> I will not gaze on glories,
>   But on my King of grace:
> Not on the crown He giveth,

But on His pierced hand:
The *Lamb* is all the glory
In Emmanuel's land.

Yes, the *Lamb* is all the glory in that fair realm where, with
sin and the curse utterly done away, Christ and his own are
one for evermore. And how wonderfully it climaxes the Bible
doctrine of the *centrality* of the Lamb! We have seen the centrality of the Lamb as set forth in Isaiah 53, and in Revelation
5, and in Revelation 21-22: the Lamb amid the throes of his
agony; the Lamb amid the throne of his glory; the Lamb amid
the throng of the glorified. We have seen him bearing our sin
on earth, wearing the crown in heaven, sharing his glory with
us forever.

Behold, then, the triune centrality of the Lamb — the Cross,
the Crown, the City. Crucifixion, Coronation, Consummation.
He is central not only in prophecy and history, not only in the
adoration of the heavenly hosts, and in the government of the
universe, but throughout the future even to "the ages of the
ages." He is the one true Savior of men, the King of kings and
Lord of lords; the Consummator of the ages, and the everlasting glory of his people. Glory to the Lamb!

Let changing theological fashions come and go. Let twen-
tieth-century cynicisms be what they may. Let men deride and
demons fume. Let oppositions multiply. The only message
which saves men is the gospel of the *LAMB*. More than ever,
the Lamb must be the center of our preaching and planning
and serving, of our faith and hope and love. More concen-
tratedly than ever let us proclaim him, uplift him, glory in him,
love him, live for him, and, if need be, die for him. And let
us beware of becoming so professionally theological, or so re-
ligiously busy, or so pragmatically antisentimental, that we do
not thrill at the prospect of seeing him at last — the "King in
his beauty, in the land of far distances." Think of it —

Not merely one glimpse, but forever,
    At home with Him, ever to be;
With Him in that glory celestial,
    Where shimmers the crystal sea:
Yet there, even there, in such glory,
    Will anything ever efface
That rapturous moment of moments,
    My first, first sight of His face!

CHAPTER THREE

THE SOVEREIGNTY OF THE LAMB

(1) Pre-incarnate

*Certainly we need to guard against any
morbid or merely sentimental dwelling on the
harrowing details of our Lord's crucifixion. Yet
perhaps there is renewed reason in these days of
unmeditating hurry why we should deliberately
pause sometimes to think what that Calvary
horror must have meant to that gentle mind and
even to that pinioned flesh of our Saviour.
The nailing of the crucified victim to the cross
was the first in a series of agonies. The second
factor causing keen suffering was the abnormal
position of the body, the slightest movement
occasioning acutest torture. A third factor
was the traumatic fever induced by hanging
for so long. Within six to twelve minutes blood
pressure would drop to 50 with pulse racing
at double rate. Under such agonizing
excruciation the heart is deprived of blood and
eventually collapses.*

— ANONYMOUS

Oh, never, never can we know
That midnight of mysterious woe
When, God-forsaken, there He cried,
And thus forlorn and pain-racked died.

THE FURTHER WE inquire into this Bible doctrine of the Lamb, the more impressive it becomes. In our first study we followed the unfolding *manifestation* of the Lamb through successive books of Holy Writ. Then, in our second survey, we saw how movingly the Bible exhibits the *centrality* of the Lamb. We now examine a further feature of the subject, namely, the Bible testimony as to the *sovereignty* of the Lamb.

The Bible reveals the sovereignty of the Lamb in three main aspects. First, there is his *preincarnate* sovereignty as the Lamb designate: the Lamb "slain from the foundation of the world" (1 Peter 1:20; Rev. 13:8). Second, there is his *postresurrection* sovereignty as the Lamb now crowned in heaven: the Lamb "in the midst of the throne" (Revelation 5). Third, there is his *never-ending* sovereignty as the Lamb destined to rule over all worlds and beings in the ages to come: the Lamb supreme amid the "new heaven and new earth" (Revelation 21, 22).

His Preincarnate Sovereignty

First we think of his sovereignty prior to his incarnation in our humanhood, that is, his sovereignty as the Lamb "fore-ordained before the foundation of the world." In this connection we turn again to the Prophet Isaiah.

In many quarters today it is fashionable to hold that our Book of Isaiah comes from a plurality of authors rather than from the one well-known Isaiah who was the ablest penman in King Hezekiah's guild of literary experts. Some of the earlier German higher critics supposedly discovered seventy or more different hands in the work, and one of them who evidently wanted to excel all his brother-dissectors in this latter-day quasi-science of literary vivisection "discovered" no less than one hundred and twenty-two authors instead of just the one Isaiah, the "son of Amoz"!

The comical peculiarity about these higher critical discoveries is that all those other penmen who had a part in the supposedly composite product which we call "the Book of Isaiah" are unidentifiable anonymities about whose existence there is not a wisp of evidence save in the fertile imaginations of the critics!

A more conservative theory now is that there were at least *two* Isaiahs — one of them the pre-Exile Isaiah of Hezekiah's day, who wrote chapters 1 to 39, the other a supposedly post-Exile, so-called "Deutero-Isaiah" who compiled chapters 40 to 66 — though once again the so-called "Deutero" is a Mr. Nobody so far as historical identification is concerned.

The rasher extravagances of the earlier higher critical detecting and dividing which reduced the Book of Isaiah to a literary patchwork quilt have been disproved by their own obvious inanity, but still today the supposition is that modern scholarship has established a greater or lesser plurality of authorship in the book, so that instead of its being strictly a "book" it is a congeries from various contributors and redactors.[1] At the very least, so it is generally supposed, there were *two* main Isaiahs, but both sections have supposedly been abundantly tinkered with by a literary class known as the Hebrew *sopherim,* or scribes, or Scripturists.

This duality (or plurality) of authorship, especially between part one (chapters 1 to 39) and part two (chapters 40 to 66) has been argued on three grounds: (1) differences of vocabulary, (2) differences of ideas and forms of expression, (3) differences in historical references and geographical background. All these have been examined and answered again and again. We need not go into them here. (For a particular examination of them I recommend Volume 3 of my *Explore the Book*).

But there is one aspect of the matter which I *do* want to mention again here, because it has been strangely neglected; that is, the overall structure of the book, which binds all its parts into one progressive whole. I make bold to submit that if only more attention had been paid to the literary *structure* and architectural *design* which are evident in this "Book of the Prophet Isaiah," its unity of authorship would have become convincingly clear, and the inventive genius of the higher critics might have been spared the need of discovering so many supposed joint-authors who never existed. Let me quickly explain what I mean.

With all other Bible students, I accept that the "Book of Isaiah" falls into those two main parts: that is, chapters 1 to 39

---

[1]In the *Cambridge Bible for Schools and Colleges* Professor Skinner wrote: "The book which bears the name of Isaiah is in reality a collection of prophetic oracles showing manifest traces of composite authorship, and having a complicated literary history behind it. Not much less than two-thirds of its bulk consists of anonymous prophecies . . . to this class belongs first of all the whole of the latter part of the book . . . but even when we confine our attention to chapters 1 to 39 we still find abundant evidence of great diversity of authorship." So there we are! — our "Book of Isaiah" is a sheer patchwork from a combination of anonymous authors whose number no one knows!

and then chapters 40 to 66, though even that needs one incidental correction. To be strictly accurate, the book is in *three* parts: (1) chapters 1 to 35, which are a complete catena of poetic prophecies in themselves; (2) chapters 36 to 39, which are *not* prophetical at all in the predictive sense: they are an *historical interlude,* and they are written in prose, not poetry; (3) chapters 40 to 66, which are one continuous messianic poem-prophecy.

If we now look carefully through the first main chain of prophecies (chapters 1 to 35) and then through the second (40 to 66) we shall find plan and pattern developing through each of them, indicating composition by one author. Also, we shall find a key chapter in each of those two series, and those two key chapters tell us something stupendous about the sovereignty of the Lamb.

Chapters 1 to 35

An observant reader will notice that chapters 1 to 6 are all confined to Judah and Jerusalem. But that sixth chapter marks a crisis. Isaiah experiences his transforming vision of Jehovah as the *King* — King of all nations and of all history, transcendent above all the convulsions of time, and reigning in sovereign, purposive control over all developments. From that point onward Isaiah's prophecies reach out, ever widening and further-seeing into the future.

The first six chapters, as noted, are limited to Judah. The next six chapters (7-12) reach out to the northern kingdom, Israel. The next eleven chapters (13-23) spread out to include ten great nations of Isaiah's own era: Babylon (13, 14), Philistia

(14:28-32), Moab (15, 16), Syria (17, 18), Egypt (19, 20), etc.

Next, in chapters 24 to 27, we have the "Day of Jehovah" in relation to the *whole world*. From special denunciations of woe on particular nations Isaiah passes to tremendous predictions involving the whole human race. Expositors uniformly agree that the language of these mighty predictions does indeed embrace the entire earth. We only need quote two or three verses.

> Behold, Jehovah maketh the earth empty . . .
> and scattereth abroad the inhabitants thereof . . .
> the *world* languisheth and fadeth away. . . . And
> it shall come to pass in that day, that Jehovah
> will punish the host of the high ones on high, and
> the kings of the earth upon the earth. . . . Jeho-
> vah of hosts will make unto all peoples a feast of
> fat things. . . . And he will destroy in this moun-
> tain the face of the covering that covereth *all
> peoples,* and the veil that is spread over *all na-
> tions.*

The dominant subject in all the chapters, so far, is the "Day of Jehovah" — a day which certainly came upon all those powers of Isaiah's pre-Christian era, but which, in coming on them, forepictured a *final* "Day of Jehovah" yet to be.

See, then, how Isaiah's outreach is broadening: first the message to Judah, then outward to Israel, then to all the surrounding Gentile nations, then to the whole world!

In chapters 28 to 33 we find a sharply distinguished group of six chapters pronouncing six "woes" on *Jerusalem,* which is ever the center of all God's earth-dealings. The city of highest privilege is the city of heaviest responsibility.

1. On drunkards of Ephraim and Judah (28)

2. Hypocrites (13) of Ariel (29:1-14)

3. Evil schemers of Jerusalem (29:15-24)

4. The revolters against Jehovah (30)

5. The unholy alliance-makers (31, 32)

6. The spoiler of Jerusalem (33)

Finally, in chapters 34 and 35, this first series of prophecies reaches its climax. The two chapters are an inseparable but sharply contrasting pair. Not only do they girdle the globe, they wing right on to the end of our present age and into the coming Millennium. They depict Jehovah's world-vengeance (34) and Zion's final restoration (35), or, in other words, the "wrath to come" at the end of this present age, and the "kingdom to come" — our Lord's global empire which crowns the history of our Adamic race. See how chapter 34 begins:

> Come near, ye nations, to hear; and hearken, ye peoples. Let the earth hear, and the fulness thereof; the world and all things that come forth from it. For Jehovah hath indignation against all the nations, and wrath against all their host. He hath utterly destroyed them; he hath delivered them to the slaughter. . . . And all the host of heaven shall be dissolved, and the heavens shall be rolled together as a scroll. . . . For Jehovah hath a day of vengeance, a year of recompence for the cause of Zion.

Thus does Isaiah carry us on, right to the fearful storm of the divine wrath which shakes all nations and all the powers of evil and culminates the present age. But in chapter 35 we are right through it and on into the glorious new day of the Millennium.

> The wilderness and the dry land shall be glad;
> and the desert shall rejoice and blossom as the
> rose. . . . The eyes of the blind shall be opened,
> and the ears of the deaf shall be unstopped.
> Then shall the lame man leap as a hart, and the
> tongue of the dumb shall sing. . . . And the
> ransomed of Jehovah shall return and come with
> singing unto Zion; and everlasting joy shall be
> upon their heads: they shall obtain gladness and
> joy, and sorrow and sighing shall flee away!

Yes, that is the millennial climax. How remarkable, then, is the expanding development in this first part of Isaiah! Glance back again. In the first six chapters we are limited to Judah, but after that transforming vision in chapter 6, the prophecies reach out more and more until they have comprehended all nations and all history!

See it in vivid summary: the first six chapters, Judah only. The next six chapters, the ten-tribed Israel. The next group of chapters, all the main kingdoms of Isaiah's era. Then, in the next group the whole world is revolving before the eye of prophecy. Next, in chapters 28 to 33, Jerusalem becomes the focus-point as being the center of all Jehovah's controversy and ultimate purpose with the nations of our earth. Finally, in chapters 34 and 35, we are plunged into the age-end "great tribulation," and then brought through to the golden climax of the Millennium! Is not that indeed wonderful expansion, development, progress, design? And does it not argue *one* human author behind the whole of it? — even as it also indicates the one *divine* Author behind the human?

How much more meaningful becomes that sixth chapter with its overwheming vision of Jehovah as King of all nations and ages — the vision which turned a parochial scribe into a world-wide prophet of God, with a clarion voice reverberating through centuries right on to the end of time!

Chapter 40—66

But now we turn to that other weighty scroll of the prophet's oracles: Isaiah 40 through 66. Here, as presented in our English versions, we have twenty-seven chapters, and in them there is evident plan and pattern as much as in the earlier set of prophecies.

These twenty-seven chapters taken collectively shape themselves into one developing messianic poem-prophecy, and there is a significant grouping of the twenty-seven into three groups of nine chapters each, the end of each group being marked off by the same solemn refrain. At the end of the first nine (48:22) we read: "There is no peace, saith Jehovah, to the wicked." At the end of the second nine (57:21) we read: "There is no peace, saith my God, to the wicked." Finally, at the end of the third nine (66:24) we have the same in an amplified form: "Their worm shall not die, neither shall their fire be quenched. . . ."

In the first nine the accent is on the *supremacy* of Jehovah; in the second nine, the *servant* of Jehovah; in the third nine, the *challenge* of Jehovah.[2] The middle nine consists of chapters 49 to 57. So the middle chapter of that middle nine is chapter 53, which by common consent is the greatest of all Old Testament passages on the expiatory and atoning sufferings of our Lord Jesus. And in the exact center of that fifty-third chapter we find,

He is led as a Lamb to the slaughter.

Is that arresting singularity merely another coincidence? To

---

[2]For more details on this see *Explore the Book,* Volume 3, by the author.

some, no doubt, nothing more. But think of it: one long, messianic poem-prophecy consisting of twenty-seven chapters, self-punctuated into three groups of nine chapters each — and the middle chapter of the middle nine the great Sin-bearer chapter — and the middle couplet of that center-most chapter:

> *He is led as a Lamb to the slaughter, and as a sheep before its shearers . . .*

Shall we insist on calling it sheer accident that in this orderly, progressive poem-prophecy the *Lamb* is thus put at dead-center in the middle chapter of the middle nine? Are we not meant to see one more peculiarly captivating indication that the *Lamb* is the crux, the vital focus, the very heart and center of God's message to man? That fifty-third chapter is the *hub* around which the whole wheel of Isaiah's message of coming redemption revolves.

How can we ever read that fifty-third chapter of Isaiah without tears of grief and shouts of wondering praise? Oh, the mystery of that profound and agonizing substitution! Oh, the wonder of that glorious love which endured for us that immeasurable woe! Amid the shifting sands of human speculation, and despite the popular new philosophies of our time, we must keep the *Lamb* at the very center of our message. We are not preaching mere religion, or philosophy, or some novelty that panders to modern thought. We are preaching the one and only authentic *revelation of God,* and the one and only true *redemption of man.* At the very center of that revelation and redemption is the *Lamb.* There is no other Savior, and there is no other salvation. We must keep the Lamb where God has put him — utterly central — in our faith and hope and love, in our preaching and testifying, in all our planning and Christian enterprise.

Even that, however, is not the final significance of Isaiah's focus on the Lamb. All that we have seen so far, in his two

series of prophecies, rises to its supreme meaning when we compare the two key chapters in those two series. As we saw, the
key or pivot in the *first* series (1—35) is chapter 6 with its
electrifying vision of the heavenly throne, from which point the
prophecies so spectacularly expand. The key chapter in the
second series (40—66) is that central fifty-third chapter; the
Lamb chapter.

First Key-Chapter

Reflect again for a moment on those two chapters. The
opening words of chapter 6 are very familiar to most of us, but
it is good to pause anew and try to visualize realistically what
Isaiah describes.

In the year that king Uzziah died I saw the Lord,
sitting upon a throne, high and lifted up; and his
train filled the temple. Above him stood the
seraphim: each one had six wings; with twain he
covered his face, and with twain he covered his
feet, and with twain he did fly. And one cried
unto another, and said, Holy, holy, holy is Jehovah of hosts: the whole earth is full of his
glory. And the foundations of the thresholds
shook at the voice of him that cried, and the
house was filled with smoke. Then said I: Woe
is me! for I am undone; because I am a man of
unclean lips, and I dwell in the midst of a people of unclean lips: for mine eyes have seen
the King, Jehovah of hosts!

The vision soars to its high point in that awed exclamation, "Mine eyes have seen *the King, Jehovah of Hosts!*" There was the glory-flashing throne "high and lifted up," and the royal "train" filling the heavenly temple (or palace), and "the King" — even *Jehovah of Hosts,* the Creator and Controller of the universe. There were the fire-like "seraphs," or "burning ones," crying, "Holy, holy, holy is Jehovah of hosts" — at which cry the very "foundations" moved, as though the whole building was awed into trembling, and the house became "filled with smoke," as though even the heavenly temple or palace sought to veil itself, as the six-winged seraphs did.

But the two predominant impressions which prostrated Isaiah were those of sin-exposing holiness and all-transcendent *sovereignty.* It was a sight of sheer glory and absolute super-control. Supreme over the histories and destinies of all nations and peoples Isaiah saw that flaming super-throne and the all-controlling purpose of a sovereign omnipotence. That was the strongest impact of the vision. All the globe-circling, history-spanning prophecies which later flowed from Isaiah's pen were implicit in that one terrific sight of the universe's *King.*

That overpowering apocalypse, however, assumes an even more eloquent splendor from the New Testament comment upon it. In John 12:41 we read: "These things said Isaiah because he saw *his* [i.e. *Christ's*] glory, and spake of *him.*" When young Isaiah saw "the Lord" (Hebrew, *Adonay*) he was beholding the preincarnate "Son of Man"!

Second Key-Chapter

And now turn to that other key-chapter, Isaiah 53, the Lamb

chapter. "Who hath believed our report? And to whom is the arm of Jehovah revealed? . . ." Remarkably enough, that twelfth chapter of John, just quoted, which says that it was our Lord Jesus Christ who was on the heavenly throne in Isaiah 6, tells us equally clearly that it was our Lord Jesus whom Isaiah saw as the atoning Sufferer in chapter 53. See John 12:37, 38: "But though he had done so many signs before them, yet they believed not on him: that the word of Isaiah might be fulfilled which he spake: Lord, who hath believed our report?"

The marvel which staggered Isaiah was that the despised, rejected, humiliated, bruised, wounded, pierced, broken, un-resisting, meek and lowly, suffering Sin-bearer whom he saw "led as a lamb to the slaughter" was the very One whom he had earlier seen surrounded by overwhelming heavenly splendor, sitting on the glory-flashing throne, reigning in super-sovereignty over all nations and centuries! His omnipotent sovereignty which could crush a million alpha-stars underfoot and never feel them; that sovereignty with its blaze of sin-consuming holiness which could burn up the whole race of human sinners in instantaneous extinction; that eternal sovereignty which governs all worlds and all beings; *that* sovereignty incarnates itself in the person of *Jesus,* descends from that ineffable throne of glory, and hangs on that gory, felon's Cross as the *Lamb* which bears away the sin of the world!

That diademed Prince of glory, hanging in shame on that fearful Cross is the most astonishing thing which ever happened in the history of the universe, or in the life of the un-created Creator himself! How can we ever be anything other than "lost in wonder, love, and praise"?

> Wonder of wonders! Vast surprise!
> Could bigger wonder be,
> That He who built the starry skies
> Once bled and died for me?

> Amazing, startling sacrifice,
>   Confounding all our thought!
> Stupendous, staggering purchase-price
>   Which our redemption bought!

The Sovereign of all becomes the Sin-bearer of all! The regal Lion becomes the bleeding Lamb! The most baffling spectacle which angel hosts ever saw was that almighty divine sovereignty fastened by iron spikes to a criminal's cross on this earth. So, then, in Isaiah see the sovereignty of the Lamb: reigning as King over all, then hanging on a Cross as Savior of all. What a Savior!

CHAPTER FOUR

THE SOVEREIGNTY OF THE LAMB

---

(2) Post-resurrection

It was one of the immeasurable evils which
the Roman Church inflicted on Christendom,
that it held constantly before the eyes of the
Church the exhausted, suffering, agonized form
of Christ on the Cross — fastened the
thought and imagination of Christian men on
the extremity of His mortal weakness, and so
deprived them of the animation and the courage
inspired by the knowledge that He is now on the
throne of the Eternal. A similar loss may
be inflicted on ourselves if our thoughts are im-
prisoned within the limits of the earthly life of
Christ, and if we do not exult in His resurrection
and in His constant presence in the Church.
The historic Christ is the Object of memory:
the present, the living Christ, is the Object of
faith, the Source of power, the Inspiration of
love, the Author of salvation.

— R. W. DALE

IT IS TIME now to turn from the poetic oracles of Isaiah to the Patmos apocalypse of John, in the last book of our Bible. If in Isaiah we have a heart-moving *preview* of the suffering Lamb, in the Book of Revelation we have the soul-stirring *sequel.*

We should be paying special attention to the Book of Revelation just now. Unless many of us are strangely mistaken, history on this earth is now quickly moving into that age-end convulsion and transition to a new global order which the Book of Revelation largely forepictures to us.

Many among us have the idea that the Book of Revelation is mostly a mystifying riddle of cryptic signs and uninterpretable symbols. That is a pity, for it is the one book of Holy Writ which is actually named a *"Revelation"!* A revelation is meant to reveal and to be understood. Perhaps some of us are so busy imagining hidden meanings everywhere in it that we miss the big simplicities which are plainly written.

Admittedly, many of the apocalyptic visions *do* have symbols which are purposely enigmatic for the time being, and which wait to be eventually unlocked by recognized fulfillment, but in its overall meaning and focal message the Book of the Revelation is one of the plainest parts of Holy Writ. No book of Scripture develops according to a clearer plan. It runs in three main movements, and those three movements issue in three successive enthronements — three enthronements of the *Lamb*. In fact, the Book of Revelation might well be called the book of the three enthronements. Let me open up those three movements a little.

First Enthronement

The first movement runs through chapters 1 through 5. Observe the progress in it. In chapter 1 we have the vision of the risen and glorified Son of Man amid the lampstands. What is the essential truth symbolized in it? Clearly, we are meant to see *Christ in heaven operating through the church on earth*. Then come chapters 2 and 3, with their brief, concentrated letters of appraisal, correction, and instruction to the seven churches. What is the predominant meaning? Surely it is that of *the church on earth functioning for the Christ in heaven*. Thus, the vision of the Son of Man amid the lampstands and the letters to the seven churches are the converse sides of the one great truth. In the one case it is the heavenward aspect: in the other, the earthward. In the first, it is Christ in heaven operating through the church on earth; in the other, the church on earth functioning for the Christ in heaven.

Our Lord, then, is risen. He operates through the church on earth. What is his last word to the church? It is this: "To him that overcometh will I grant to sit with me in my throne, even as I also overcame, and *sat down with my Father in his throne*" (3:21). This reference to our Lord's joint occupancy of the throne in heaven opens the door to the great vision of chapters 4 and 5. Chapter 4 spends itself in describing the throne of the Deity and the worship of heaven. In a word, we are shown the

place of *supreme authority* — the "throne." Then comes chapter 5, the chapter of the Lamb and the seven-sealed book, in
which we see the Lamb himself put amid the throne. The ruling
purpose in this first movement of the Apocalypse is to put the
Lamb there — in that throne of all-transcendent sovereignty.
The book cannot continue until it has shown us the Lamb *there*.
So this first movement reaches its climax with the Lamb in the
place of supreme control.

What is the prime significance of the fifth chapter and its
enthroning of our Lord Jesus in that seat of universal authority?
It is a tremendous truth which all of us ought to see clearly, but
which we easily miss if we allow preoccupation with details to
obscure the main meanings. Read the first few verses again:

> And I saw in the right hand of him that sat on
> the throne a book written within and on the back,
> close-sealed with seven seals. And I saw a
> strong angel proclaiming with a great voice: Who
> is worthy to open the book, and to loose the
> seals thereof? And no one in the heaven, or on
> the earth, or under the earth, was able to open
> the book, or to look thereon. And I wept much
> because no one was found worthy to open the
> book, or to look thereon. But one of the elders
> saith unto me: Weep not; behold, the Lion that
> is of the tribe of Judah, the Root of David, hath
> overcome to open the book and the seven seals
> thereof.

As we noted in our former study, the seven-sealed scroll is
obviously not the book of the now-open past, nor of the now-
opening present. It has to do with the future. We learn its
contents soon afterward in pictorial form, as the Lamb successively opens the seven seals. It is the book of final issues, of

God's ultimate purposes with the Adamic human race, and with the nation Israel, and with the redeemed people of Christ. It is the book which tells how the enigmatic mystery of man's sin-cursed history will eventually be cleared up. So we need not be surprised at John's weeping because no one was found "worthy" to open the book. His tears were those of godly anxiety.

The loud challenge resounds in earth and skies: "Who is worthy to open the book?" The question is really tantamount to "Who is worthy to sit in that throne of supreme authority as the *executive administrator* of the divine purposes?" or "Who is worthy of such all-controlling sovereignty?" Therefore, apart from our Lord Jesus, none was found worthy anywhere in the universe.

But are there not myriads of unfallen, sinless angels? Is there not one among all of *them* who is worthy? What of archangel Michael? What of the illustrious angel Gabriel? What of all the other high-ranking intelligences among the "morning stars of heaven"? Is there not one among all those princes of light who is worthy to open that book? What of the seraphim, or cherubim, those exalted beings of flaming holiness who seem to be nearer the throne of the ineffable Deity than all other creatures? Are *they* not "worthy?" The answer is: No, not one among all those unsullied, resplendent heavenly hosts has the peculiar qualifications which would make him "worthy" to break the seals of that mystery scroll.

What, then, are the unique qualifications which give our Lord Jesus his absolutely solitary worthiness to reveal and execute the plan and purposes of the Almighty? They are principally three.

First there is the worthiness of his incomparable *moral conquest*. See verse 5 again: "Weep not; behold, the Lion that is of the tribe of Judah, the Root of David, *overcame*."[1] That past tense, *"overcame,"* refers to our Lord's victory over sin and Satan here on earth. It was not in the omnipotent power of his Godhead that our Lord defeated the mighty tempter (which would have been easy for the omnipotent One), but in the moral power of his *manhood,* as man's new champion against the usurper. From that first major temptation in the wilderness, when, although he was at the point of collapse through protracted hunger, he would not risk getting out of the Father's will by turning the stones into food, right on to the last agony of temptation in Gethsemane when he cried to the Father, "Nevertheless, not my will, but thine be done," he *conquered*. As our Champion David he laid Goliath Satan low. In our Lord's holy *manhood* Satan had at last met more than his match. In the "meek and lowly" Jesus he met the "stronger than the strong." The utter simplicity and transparent purity of that holy manhood proved stronger than all the dark-minded duplicity of the deceiver. The archfiend had reached his Waterloo. His power over man was broken. The future banishment of Beelzebub-Apollyon was assured. For the first time in human history the serpent's head was crushed. And it was "the Man, Christ Jesus" who did it. None of the unfallen myriads of "angels and principalities and powers" of the heavenly regions has *that* worthiness! As the solitary conqueror of sin and Satan, Jesus alone is "worthy"!

But besides his being "worthy" by virtue of moral conquest, our Lord Jesus is "worthy" as the purchaser of *costly redemption*. See verse 9 again: "They sing a new song, saying: Thou

---

[1] It is unfortunate that the A.V., E.R.V., A.S.V., and R.S.V. all render the Greek aorist in this verse as a present perfect: "hath overcome," which suggests that the overcoming was somehow at the time of the vision. The true translation of the aorist here is "over*came*"; and, of course, it repeats our Lord's own word in chapter 3:21, "Even as I also *overcame*," referring to what happened when he was on earth as "the second Adam," our new Champion.

art worthy to take the book and to open the seals thereof; for thou wast slain and didst purchase unto God with thy blood men of every tribe and tongue and people and nation." Not only is he Satan's Vanquisher; he is mankind's *Redeemer,* and he is so at the cost of his own voluntary sin-bearing and unspeakable humiliation. Among all the sinless, shining hosts of heaven, none but Jesus has *that* worthiness!

And in addition to that, our Lord Jesus is alone the "worthy" One by reason of his infinite *governmental capacity.* Consider verse 6 again: "I saw in the midst of the throne . . . a Lamb, having seven horns and seven eyes which are the seven spirits of God sent forth into all the earth." As we observed in our earlier study, the seven horns symbolize *omnipotence* and the seven eyes, *omniscience,* and the seven spirits encompassing the whole earth, *omnipresence.* Those are not only superhuman and super-angelic qualities; they are exclusively *divine* attributes. The only one who can be "worthy" to open that fateful scroll of future history and destiny is one who, besides being uniquely supreme in moral conquest and in redemptive achievement, is commensurately "worthy" in constitutional capacity. Here on earth many a man who has been *morally* worthy of being a king has lacked the personal gifts and force which are necessary to true rulership. But our Lord Jesus is the absolutely "worthy" One because he conjoins with his incomparable moral conquest and redemptive self-sacrifice the possession of *infinite capacity*: omnipotence, omniscience, omnipresence. None can withstand his power. None can escape his all-seeing eye. None can elude his infallible knowledge. None can evade his ubiquitous presence.

Grasp it firmly: those are the three ways in which our dear Lord is the Lamb-Lion, the solitarily "worthy" One. (1) He is the Vanquisher of Satan; (2) he is the Redeemer of Man; (3) he is the incarnation of God. As such he *"overcame"* to open the book and to loose the seals thereof.

The mighty wonder is that when John looks to see a lion, he

sees a lamb; and that "Lamb" — alive yet bearing evidence of having been slain — is on that throne of thrones! That is the all-eclipsing biblical picture of the divine sovereignty. You and I are meant to see on the throne of the universe, this very day, God in the form of that *Man,* the Lion ruling there as the *Lamb,* the Judge who is none other than the *Redeemer,* and the divine sovereignty sublimated in *saviorhood.* When I see the Lamb *there,* I am no longer afraid of the universe or of the unknown future or of what lies on the other side of the shadowy grave. With the Lamb there, on that throne, the universe is safe, the future is guaranteed, and beyond the grave there are assured fulfillments which will rectify the frustrations of this sin-spoiled present. The baffling mystery of permitted evil is answered by the absolute mastery of the Lamb in the throne. The dragon's days are numbered! A "new earth" is on its way! The whole universe shall yet sing, "He hath done all things well!"

Some years ago I was invited to become the minister of a large church in U.S.A. The invitation was warmly worded, but it contained the following question: "Do you fully hold the doctrines of sovereign grace?" Not long afterward another church, wanting a series of special Bible-teaching gatherings, asked me the same question: "Do you go all the way with the doctrines of sovereign grace?"

It is a great phrase: "sovereign grace" (though I am not sure it is always used in just the way John Calvin meant!). What *is* "sovereign grace"? If we would see it in its most vivid meaning we need to rivet our minds on those three chapters: Isaiah 6, Isaiah 53, and Revelation 5. We need to take a long, thoughtful look at the preincarnate Christ of Isaiah 6, high on that exquisite throne of universal empire amid the blaze of heaven's glory-light. Then we need to turn our intent gaze upon that same Lord of glory descending from his peerless sovereignty in chapter 6 to that blood and shame and suffering and substitutionary sin-bearing in chapter 53. That is *sover-*

eignty becoming "grace"! Then we need to watch and wonder as that willingly slaughtered Lamb, the lowly "Son of Man," conquers death and ascends to that all-transcendent throne again, carrying there his now-glorified manhood as the Representative of the countless millions he has redeemed. As we see him, the Lamb of Calvary, thus reoccupying that throne of universal dominion, we see *grace* becoming *"sovereign."* Yes, that is "sovereign grace"; and that is why that throne is now called in Scripture, "the throne of grace" (Heb. 4:16).

We Christian believers, and especially those of us who are public spokesmen of the faith, are needing a new vision of that "sovereign grace" today. No man whose inward eyes have really seen that overwhelmingly holy Christ in Isaiah 6 ever talks again about his own sanctity. No man who has ever really seen with his *soul* that bruised, broken, bleeding, disfigured Sufferer in Isaiah 53 ever talks of himself again. No man who has ever really "seen" the revolutionary meaning of that "Lamb amid the throne" in Revelation 5 is ever a pessimist or defeatist again. With Jesus on that throne, final issues are certified.

In the early phase of the Second World War, it appeared that Hitler and his Nazis would win, but a point came later when it was plain he would lose. The war dragged on for weary and costly months after that, but the outcome was no longer in doubt. Similarly, the war of light against darkness, of evil against goodness, still drags on, but since the Lamb occupied that throne of sovereign control the result is settled. The archrebel in God's universe is a beaten foe. He and his accomplices still wreak vast havoc. They sweep around us today with a new and damaging offensive. They have largely captured the radio and television. They have surged in afresh under the battle flag of the "permissive society" or "new morality." They have broken in to de-Christianize society, not by frontal attack on the Church from outside it, but through Quislings who betray it from the *inside* by undermining faith in the Bible. They

have launched a mighty offensive of anti-Godism through the
global outreach of Communism. But if Satan is flinging away
disguise and ravaging as a beast of prey today, it is because the
age is nearly over, and he "knoweth that he hath but a short
time" (Rev. 12:12). The Lamb is on the throne. Soon, now,
he will tread all rebels to the dust in everlasting obliteration.
I say again: we are needing a new vision of all this. I used
to be suspicious of visions and the visionary type of person.
Perhaps I still am. Many so-called visions are products of high-
strung imagination or of emotional excitement, and some people are peculiarly prone to them. But there is a kind of vision
which is healthily different from all that. It is not optical and
transient, but spiritual and lasting. It is no figment of autosug-
gestion, but is powerfully luminous to the mind and sanctifying
in one's character. The mind "sees" and grasps something in
such a way that life is never quite the same again. I believe
our Lord had some such revealing of himself to our minds when
he said, "He that hath my commandments and keepeth them,
he it is that loveth me; and he that loveth me shall be loved
of my Father; and I will love him, and will *manifest* myself
unto him" (John 14:21).

Living as we are in times of unprecedented abnormality and
chaotic mental confusion, if we are to be true prophets of our
Lord to the present generation we need such a vision. We
need to *see* that throne of flaming holiness until we are prostrated in awed adoration. We need to *see* that dear Savior on
Calvary until the wonder of his great love melts us into lifelong
surrender. We need to *see* that "Lamb in the midst of the
throne" until the absolute sovereignty of the Lamb dominates
all our thinking about the world, about history, about the future, and lives with us day after day.

The marvel of marvels is that the sovereignty of the universe's Creator is exercised through the *Lamb*. In terms of
earthly time-reckoning, God put him on the throne two thousand years ago. All other figures of history pale into insignifi-

cance. Despite all temporary appearances to the contrary in the present hour, the decisions of world government, the disposing of history, and the destinies of nations are all in the controlling hand of our sovereign Lord Jesus. That includes prodigal-son America, turning away from the godly convictions of its founding fathers, and wasting its wealth in riotous fleshliness. It also includes Gog, alias the Prince of Resh, red Russia, with its mail-fisted tyranny and iron-curtain empire. It also includes the vast land of Sinim, the new China, with its seven hundred millions of brain-washed Communists.

That is not mere rhetorical hyperbole: we are declaring the most stupendous reality of the centuries. All earth's billions are in those hands which were once spiked to that rough-hewn cross on Calvary! We need to *"see"* it all with new mental clearness, and proclaim it with eager, undiscouraged insistence.

I sometimes wonder whether in our overseas missionary outreach and in our evangelism at home we have slipped away somewhat from the central emphasis of the New Testament. We keep telling men (and rightly so) that they *need* something, but the central emphasis of the New Testament is that *God* in sovereign grace has *done* something — something which all men have a right to know. He did it once for all, and for all men. He did it in the person of his eternal Son — born as a babe at Bethlehem, crucified as the world's Sin-bearer on Calvary, and now exalted as our glorious Brother-Man and Representative in that all-sovereign throne of heaven. We are to tell men now, not so much that they are born into a lost world, but into a lost world which has been saved; that all of us have a God-given inheritance in that effected salvation, and that

> None are excluded thence but they
> Who do themselves exclude.

One of our Savior's words after rising from the dead was: *"All authority* is given unto me in heaven and on earth," and it was on the basis of that all-comprehending sovereignty that he sent his disciples to "preach the glad news to every creature." *That* is "sovereign grace." That is the Church's central and continuous message. The Lamb who died on that cross *now reigns on that throne.*

Second Enthronement

But now, with that in mind, follow on through the second main movement of the Apocalypse, the object of which is to crown our Lord Jesus on the throne as sole Emperor *here on earth.* In Revelation 6 to 11 our Lord successively unlooses the seven seals of the mysterious scroll. When he breaks open the seventh there appear "seven angels" having "seven trumpets." The climax is reached when the seventh trumpet sounds, ending the intense three-and-a-half years called the "wrath of the *Lamb*" (6:16) and the "wrath of *God*" (11:18 with 14:10, 19, etc.).

> The seventh angel sounded; and there followed great voices in heaven, and they said: The world-kingdom of our Lord and of his Christ has come; and he shall reign for ever and ever (11:15).

Chapters 12 to 19 then amplify various aspects of that three-and-a-half year "wrath" period, and then climax in a more detailed account showing *how* the world-kingdom of the Lamb is brought in. This is how the whole movement heads up in the nineteenth chapter:

> And I heard as it were the voice of a great

multitude, and as the voice of many waters, and as the voice of mighty thunders, saying: Hallelujah, for the Lord our God, the Almighty reigneth. Let us rejoice and be exceeding glad, and let us give the glory unto him; for the marriage of the *Lamb* is come, and his wife hath made herself ready (19:6, 7).

And I saw the heaven opened; and behold, a white horse, and he that sat thereon, called Faithful and True; and in righteousness he doth judge and make war. His eyes are a flame of fire, and upon his head are many diadems . . . and his name is called the Word of God. And the armies which are in heaven followed him upon white horses, clothed in fine linen, white and pure. And out of his mouth proceedeth a sharp sword, that with it he should smite the nations: and he shall rule them with a rod of iron: and he treadeth the winepress of the fierceness of the wrath of Almighty God. And he hath on his garment and on his thigh a name written: KING OF KINGS, AND LORD OF LORDS (19:11-16).

And I saw thrones and they [the overcomers] sat upon them, and judgment was given unto them. And I saw the souls of them that had been beheaded for the testimony of Jesus and for the Word of God, and such as had not worshipped the beast, neither his image, and received not his mark upon their forehead and upon their hand; and they lived, *and reigned with Christ a thousand years"* (20:4-6).

That this reign is indeed to be on earth is certified by six locating particulars. First: our Lord's descent as King of Kings and Lord of Lords is to this *earth,* to "smite" and then "rule" the *"nations"* (19:15). Second: the armies of "kings" and "captains" and "mighty men" are overthrown on *earth,* for the "fowls" are filled with their *"flesh"* (19:15, 18, 21). Third: Satan is bound for a thousand years, that he should no more "deceive the *nations"* until the end of that millennium (20:3). Fourth: when Satan is briefly released about the *end* of the "thousand years" he goes out again to the "four quarters of the *earth"* once again to "deceive the *nations"* (20:7, 8). Fifth: those who "live" and "reign" with Christ during the "thousand years" include those who were *"beheaded"* for his sake on earth, and they now live again *bodily,* having been physically raised in "the first *resurrection"* (20:4-6). Sixth: when Satan emerges at the *end* of the "thousand years" he gathers his insurrectionists from "the breadth of the *earth"* against the "beloved *city";* then fire comes *"down* from God *out of* heaven" and devours them (20:7-9).

Symbols or no symbols, could Scripture make it any plainer that the thousand-year reign is to be on *earth?* If, as some assert, the reign of Christ and the resurrected saints is purely spiritual, why such repeated attaching of it to the *earth?* and why does it need a resurrection of the *body* in order for the saints to participate in it? All the way through the Book of Revelation, when the wording specifically states that something will happen on the earth it *means* this earth — otherwise the book would be a farce. One of its leading purposes is to tell how things will eventuate on *this earth* at the end of the present age and afterward.

All the way through both Old and New Testament prediction, the eventual earth-rule of our Lord Jesus as the Seed of Abraham and the Son of David and the Christ of Jehovah is foretold. That earth-rule has never yet happened. It certainly is not on earth today in this time of widespread apostasy in the organized

Christian Church, catastrophic moral landslide throughout Christendom, and internationally organized anti-Godism through Russian Communism. But it yet *will* happen, unless Old and New Testament prophecy is deceptive in its most deliberate and specific assurances.

To say, as do the amillennialists, that the thousand years are the present gospel age is indeed strange exegesis! This present age is distinctively the age of *grace,* whereas in the coming millennial age our Lord shall first "smite the nations" and then "rule them with a rod of iron" (19:15). To say that this present age of Heaven's grace and permissive forbearance fulfils those predictions is surely a surprising kind of exposition!

During the thousand years of our Lord's messianic world-reign Satan is to be completely removed from the earth scene so that he cannot then any longer "deceive the nations" (20:3). Could anything make that complete removal of Satan plainer than the fivefold enactment by the angel who comes "down out of heaven, having the key of the abyss [the deepest depth of hades] and a great chain in his hand"? The angel (1) laid hold on [*ekratesen,* "overpowered"] him; (2) bound him with the great chain; (3) hurled him down into the abyss; (4) and shut it; (5) and sealed it over him.

If that fivefold build-up does not describe an utter removal and confinement of Satan, then nothing could. To make the matter even surer, however, verse 7 adds, "And when the thousand years are finished [notice that here we have direct statement, not merely a vision] Satan shall be loosed out of his *prison* [so it has been a real incarceration] and shall come forth to deceive the nations. . . ." — a final exposure of his innate incorrigibility, whereupon his deserved doom is effected. We can hardly believe our eyes when we find amillennialist brethren writing that the chaining and removing of Satan is *now,* during this age of gospel grace.

"One of the chief prohibitions laid upon him

was that he should deceive the nations no more
until the end of the period symbolized by the
thousand years *which represent the Gospel age"*
(italics mine).

"This is his present place of abode [i.e. the
abyss] from which he *carries on his activities."*

"He walks about as a roaring lion, but is a
chained lion and can go only so far as the chain
allows."

What kind of exegesis is that? What pitiful draining away
of meaning from the clear wording of Scripture! As for the
present age, Satan is not even chained, much less flung into the
abyss. Nay, as John says, "The whole world lieth in the evil
one" (1 John 5:19). And in the words of Paul, "If our gospel
be veiled, it is veiled in them that are perishing, in whom the
god of this age [this present, so-called gospel age] hath blinded
the minds of the unbelieving" (2 Cor. 4:3, 4). Nor is Satan
operating from the abyss; he is the prince of the power of the
air, "the spirit that now worketh in the sons of disobedience"
(Eph. 2:2). All the way through the New Testament we are
warned about a Satan who is terribly powerful, still free, and
everywhere active, both as an angel of light to deceive and as
a roaring lion to devour. Also, the written Word tells us that
near the end of the present age Satan is flung out of the
heavenly sphere (Rev. 12:7-10) from where he comes *down*
to this earth, (not *up* from the abyss) "having great wrath,
knowing that he hath but a short time" (v. 12).

No, this present gospel age certainly is *not* the thousand
years of Satan's banishment to the dungeon of hades, nor is it
the age of our Lord's plentifully predicted messianic empire
on earth. But that coming millennial Christocracy is just as
certainly on its way as our Lord is certainly enthroned already
in heaven as the "Lamb in the midst of the throne." And its
duration will be for the specified thousand years. One feature

which must impress any open-minded reader of Revelation 20 is the prominence given by reiteration to the time-period of a "thousand years." No less than six times the expression occurs, and in four out of the six it has the definite article — *"the thousand years"* — as though by repeated definition to fix a specific period in our minds. Moreover, in verses 6 and 7 the wording passes from description of a vision to *direct prediction*: "They *shall reign* with him the thousand years."

As we said at the beginning of these studies, one of the most impressive phenomena of the Bible is its *progress* of doctrine. One outstanding instance of such progress is the Bible doctrine of the Lamb, which we are here examining. Other examples are the progress of revelation concerning the being of God, the progress of disclosure about life beyond the grave, and the progress of prophecy on the coming messianic kingdom. One feature after another contributes to the build-up of information about the global reign of the Messiah which will consummate the history of Adam's race on this earth, until here, in Revelation 20, we are given the final information as to its *duration*.

The history of Adamic humanity on this earth thus becomes an heptadic cycle, or week, of seven great thousand-year days: four thousand years B.C., then two thousand years A.D., and finally one thousand years R.D., i.e., *Regno Domini:* in the *Reign* of the Lord." As the seventh day, this coming Millennium will be history's completive *sabbath* of worldwide, warless peace and rest. It will be so because our Lord Jesus will then be visibly back on earth and reigning as global Sovereign.

Third Enthronement

From that millennial enthronement of our Lord on earth the

Apocalyptic panorama moves on through the final insurrection and abolition of evil to the general judgment of mankind at the Great White Throne. In that awesome, immeasurably vast and fateful assize, which both congregates and yet discriminates all human beings of all the centuries before the divine Judge, the deciding factor is: "And whosoever was not found written in the book of life. . . ." That book of life is "the book of life of the *Lamb*" (Rev. 13:8; 20:27). So the Lamb is sovereign not only in the throne of heaven, and in the wrath to come, and in the future global empire, but also in racial judgment.

That judgment of the whole human race at the Great White Throne not only decides the eternal destiny of human individuals, it terminates the present world-cosmos forever. If we rightly understand the language of Scripture, there is going to be a fundamental refashioning of our earth to become the habitation of a new humanity in Christ, surrounded by heavenly spheres which have been forever freed from all evil powers. Gone forever all need for the "rod of iron"! Gone forever the curse, the blight of sin, the scourge of pain, the shadow of sorrow, the tyranny of the grave. Gone forever all frustration, weeping, sighing, aging, dying. John says, "I saw a new heaven and a new earth; for the first heaven and the first earth are passed away."

Thus begins the third and final movement of the grand Apocalypse, in which we see the enthronement of the Lamb as eternal King of God's new order on and around the earth. In the words of Tennyson, that is

> The one far-off, divine event
> To which the whole creation moves.

Let it not be lost sight of for one moment that this event brings the further coronation of our Lord Jesus as the *Lamb.* Calvary is never to be forgotten. He is the beloved *Redeemer,* "yesterday and today and unto the ages."

CHAPTER FIVE

THE SOVEREIGNTY OF THE LAMB

(3) Never-ending

*Then onward and yet onward! for dim reveal-
ings show
That systems unto systems in grand succession
grow;
That what we deemed a volume, one golden
verse may be,
One rhythmic, flowing cadence in God's great
poetry.*
                                  — FRANCIS RIDLEY HAVERGAL

*Far o'er yon horizon gleam the city towers
Where our God abideth: that fair home is ours!
Flash the walls with jasper, shine the streets with
gold,
Flows the gladdening river, shedding joys un-
told!*

                                  — HENRY ALFORD

YES, A "NEW HEAVEN and a new earth"! So our Bible not only *begins* with "Genesis," it *ends* with a "genesis": a new beginning, a re-creation. That coming new order is described in the last two chapters of the Apocalype in terms which are at once august and exquisite. The inaugural motto, uttered by a voice from the throne, and written across the new order, is: "Behold, I make all things new."

> And I saw a new heaven and a new earth: for the first heaven and the first earth are passed away; and the sea is no more. And I saw the holy city, new Jerusalem, coming down out of heaven from God, made ready as a bride adorned for her husband. And I heard a great voice out of the throne saying, Behold the tabernacle of God is with men, and he shall dwell with them, and they shall be his people, and God himself shall be with them, and be their God: and he shall wipe away every tear from their eyes; and death shall be no more; neither shall there be mourning, nor crying, nor pain, anymore: the first things are passed away. And he that sitteth on the throne said, Behold, I make all things new (Rev. 21:1-5).

Such is the introductory paragraph. It is followed by a description of the new Jerusalem, with accompanying comments on the new earthly conditions, ending at chapter 22, verse 5. Seven great "new" features stand out and captivate the mind.

1. The new heaven. "And I saw a new heaven," i.e., the terrestrial expanse and solar system.

2. The new earth. "And a new earth," i.e., the present planet, but after a fundamental refashioning.

3. The new center. "I saw the holy city, new Jerusalem, coming down out of heaven from God," i.e., to this earth.

4. The new society. "They shall be his people, and God himself shall be with them," i.e., the "nations" (24).

5. The new worship. "No temple therein" — no need of one when there is open vision of the Shekinah and the Lamb.

6. The new light. "No need of sun." "The glory of God illumes it." "The nations walk in the light thereof."

7. The new paradise. "He showed me . . . the tree of life." "The fruit . . . leaves for the healing of the nations."

This is that ultimate splendor and complete felicity into which our Lord's millennial reign eventually merges. Notice that it is all *on this earth*. However common the idea may be among Christian believers, we must never think that when the history of our fallen human race is over, we Christian believers will then be millions of bodiless spirits living in a purely spiritual sphere. If that were our intended future, what purpose would there be in the coming resurrection of the *body?* Is it not to give us supernal bodies, after the pattern of our Lord's resurrection body, fitted for a higher quality of life and service in that new heaven and new earth — yes, and in those ages to come (Eph. 1:7) which lie beyond the reach of all the Apocalyptic descriptions?

Nor must we mistakenly suppose that our Bible teaches any such eventuality as "the end of the world" — at least not in the sense of the obliteration or disappearance of the *earth.* Whether or not this tiny planet of ours will pass into nothingness at some future point is not revealed in Scripture. That phrase, "the end of the world" certainly does occur in our standard English translations of the New Testament (e.g., Matt. 28:20), but as every informed reader knows, the Greek word translated as "world" is *aion* (Anglicized into "aêon" or "eon"), and means, more exactly, "the end of the *age.*" The Bible nowhere speaks of the end of the *earth.* It does say that the earth in its present condition will be "dissolved," or "burnt up," but that is preparatory to its becoming again refashioned into a "new earth," with a new "genesis" of occupation and history.

Let me repeat for emphasis: it is erroneous to think that after the all-inclusive judgment at the Great White Throne (Rev. 20:11-15) brings to an end the drama of our fallen human race, the earth will then go spinning *unoccupied* through space for ages until it gradually disintegrates into non-existence. Listen to Isaiah 45:18 again: "Thus saith Jehovah that created the heavens, God that formed the earth and made it; he established it; he created it not a waste; he formed it *to be inhabited.*"

In the coming new order there will be on this earth the most wonderful *cosmos,* or world-system, which it has ever yet known. It is to be that which is described in Revelation 21 and 22. If anyone should say that we are unduly literalizing something which is a *vision,* and not actual prediction, we reply that the same dissolution and re-creation is taught in direct statement elsewhere in Scripture. The following passage is representative:

> But the day of the Lord will come as a thief, in the which the heavens shall pass away with a great noise, and the elements shall be dissolved with fervent heat, and the earth and the works that are therein shall be burned up. . . . But, according to his promise, we look for *new heavens and a new earth* wherein dwelleth righteousness (2 Peter 3:10-13).

Peter's statement is a plain prediction of that coming "new heaven and new earth" which are pictured to us in Revelation 21 and 22. Furthermore, in John's own Patmos vision of it he recurrently passes from the visional description of it to direct statement. For instance:

> He that overcometh shall inherit these things (21:7).

> The nations shall walk in the light of it (21:24).

> They shall bring the glory and honor of the nations into it (21:26).

> There shall be no curse any more: and the throne of God and of the Lamb shall be in it (22:3).

These are some of the plain foretellings which accompany John's vision and which settle how we are to *understand* the vision.

This advance unveiling of that new heaven and new earth which are yet to be may well fascinate us, though it need not surprise us. Away back in the opening verses of Genesis we are told that before the earth was adapted for man's occupancy it was "without form and void." Yet Isaiah 45:18, already quoted, says: "God created it *not* without form" (or waste, the same word as in Genesis 1:2). So the earth must have *become* waste and void at some point after its original creation.

How and when did it become so? Where the written Word does not give us definite statement let us tread warily; yet on the other hand let us not hesitate to follow clear pointers. We cannot digress here to discuss Lucifer's relationship to this planet. From a variety of Scripture references (further comment on this later) it would seem that in a long-ago, pre-Adamite age this earth was under the overlordship of Lucifer, who by his vain infidelity and duplicity not only forfeited his position as "prince of this world," but involved a world-full of others in his downfall, occasioning the cataclysmic judgment by which the earth became "without form and void."

Until recently, modern science has rejected the idea of any such cataclysmic epoch in our planet's history, and has held that it reached its present state by a gradual, unbroken evolution. However, that is now doubted or discarded by many. One of the most recent hypotheses is that there have been a succession of such cataclysms.

After the Luciferian revolt, the desolated earth was refashioned to become the abode of mankind, as described in the "six days" of Genesis 1. How *long* after, we do not know, but the earth was now put under the lordship of man (Ps. 8:6 etc.). Thereupon Lucifer-Satan by subtle deception contrived man's fall, with all the pitiful havoc which has ensued. The archfiend usurper at length met his defeat. Our Lord Jesus, by incarnation the "Second Adam," overcame all the tempter's wiles and powers. Then, as the sinless Sinbearer, he made complete atonement on Calvary for the sin of the whole Adamic race; after which he rose in irresistible triumph over the grave, with this announcement: "All authority is [now] given unto *me,* in heaven and on earth."

Our Lord Jesus, as "Son of Man" and as "the Lamb slain from the foundation of the world," is the world's *true* "Prince and Savior" (Acts 2:32-36; 5:31). The "mystery" of permitted evil will run its course to the end of the present age, when our glorified Lord Jesus, as the Head of the *new* humanity, will return to earth in absolute command, and reign in millennial world-rule. Then, after the final judgment of mankind at the Great White Throne, instead of another long, dark interval "without form and void," the ages-to-ages reign of God and the Lamb will go on from glory to glory, Satan and all evil having been banished for ever.

It is in that new heaven and new earth that our ultimate destiny lies as the redeemed people of Christ, and as the members of his mystical body, the Church. What we are told about it therefore becomes of captivating interest. Some of its aspects are full of surprise. One is the far-reaching perpetuity of the Israel nation. The twelve gates of the new Jerusalem are inscribed, respectively, with the names of the twelve tribes of Israel (21:12, 13). The twelve foundations of the city bear the names of the twelve Apostles — one name on each (21:14). It would seem that the Abrahamic covenant and messianic prophecies reach right on to an ultimate sublimation in that flawless "new heaven and new earth."

Another surprise is the presence of "nations" and "kingdoms" in that eternal regime (21:24), all revering the new Jerusalem and the throne of the Lamb as the divinely adorned center of the new cosmos.

It further appears that the new humanity — that fair society of "the pure in heart" — will use a form of time-reckoning like that of the present solar system, if the word "months" in Revelation 22:2 has a literal meaning.

Again, since "death shall be no more" there is to be immortality, while the "tree of life," then available to all, bears fruit continuously for the healing, i.e., the continual *health,* of all peoples.

Apparently, too, there is to be a blending of the natural and the supernatural, for at the center of that new global organization, the queen city is not dependent on either sun or moon for light. The divine Presence gently floods it with Shekinah glory-light. That benign, soft radiance never tires the eyes of the immortals who live in it; so there is never any need for relief such as darkness now affords; and therefore "there shall be no night there" (21:25).

The sovereign, central magnet of it all is our Lord Jesus as the glorified *Lamb.* All who live in it know that they owe it all to him and his glorious love. It is all *his,* and his joy is to make it all *theirs.* It is the fulfillment of his prayer in John 17. In that prayer he speaks to the Father about "the glory which I had with thee before the world was" (v. 5); but later he speaks of "the glory which thou hast given me" (v. 24). The former was his preincarnate divine glory as God the Son, the Father's Co-equal. The latter is the glory given by the Father to our Lord as the guileless, stainless, sinless Son of Man, the utterly yielded Sinbearer of the human race. Up from hades and the grave God raised that spotless Victim-Victor, and exalted that resurrected manhood to the very throne of the universe! *That* is the glory which the Father has *"given"* him as "the New Man."

But now, as we think of the latter glory which the Father has "given" him, let us grasp with clearer understanding the meaning of verse 22: "And the glory which thou hast given *me,* I have given *them"!* It is in the new heaven and new earth that those words of our Lord will reach their rapture of fulfillment. The glory which the Father has given him, he will share to the full with us, through endless ages!

It is *then,* in those ages to come, and *there,* in that new heaven and new earth, that we shall drink in the full meaning of John 1:16: "Of his fullness have we all received, and grace upon grace" (i.e. successive accessions of grace). The New Testament speaks again and again about the divine grace. It also speaks about "abundance of grace," and the "glory of his grace," and the "riches of his grace." But there is only one place where we find the lavish expression, "The *exceeding* riches of his grace." It is in Ephesians 2:7, and it refers not to the present age, nor even to the millennial age to come, but to those ages upon ages *beyond* the Millennium, in that "new heaven and new earth."

> He [God] quickened us together with Christ (by grace have ye been saved) and raised us up with him, and made us to sit with him in the heavenlies, in Christ Jesus; that in the *ages to come* he might show the *exceeding riches* of his grace in his kindness toward us in Christ Jesus.

Those ages to come are also called the "ages of the ages," meaning "age upon age as far as the farthest-seeing eye can peer." Perhaps it is then and there, when the New Jerusalem and its new peoples comprise the sinless future society on earth — when there is open fellowship of heaven with earth's occupants — that we shall at last understand Jehovah's word to Israel long ago:

> . . . visiting the iniquity of the fathers upon the children to the third and fourth generation of them that hate me; but showing lovingkindness unto a *thousand generations* in them that love me and keep my commandments (Exodus 20:5, 6).

> Know therefore that Jehovah thy God, he is God, the faithful God, who keepeth covenant and lovingkindness with them that love him and

keep his commandments, to a *thousand generations* (Deut. 7:9).

Think of those words and then turn again to Ephesians 3:
21, where the apostle, with his gaze on those ages to come,
uses that word, "generations," in a way which occurs nowhere
else in the New Testament.

> Now unto him that is able to do exceeding abun-
> dantly above all that we ask or think, according
> to the power that worketh in us; unto him be
> the glory in the Church and in Christ Jesus unto
> *all the generations of the ages of the ages.*

Think of it: "all the *generations* of the ages of the ages"!
One golden age gives birth to another in a never-never-ending
progress of blessedness beyond all that we can now imagine —
until the whole history of the human race now on earth becomes
a mere dot in the past.

We must add no more. Our pen runs away with us! But see
how the Apocalyptic vision of it *ends,* in Revelation 22:3-5.

> And there shall be no curse any more: and the
> throne of God and of the *Lamb* shall be therein:
> and his servants shall serve him; and they shall
> see his face; and his name shall be on their fore-
> heads. And there shall be night no more; and
> they need no light of lamp, neither light of sun;
> for the Lord God shall give them light: and they
> shall reign unto the ages of the ages.

It is the most wonderful conceivable climax and prospect.
The more one's mind lingers over it, clause by clause, the
more it shines with an opalescent radiance which has no parallel on earth. Every facet flashes with a rapture which our

present modes of thinking are incapable of comprehending. It pictures a future state in which every lovely aspiration will be realized, and in which every high capacity of our being will be fulfilled to the uttermost. Pick out the seven ultimate perfections which are indicated in that final paragraph.

1. Perfect sinlessness — "There shall be no curse any more."

2. Perfect government — "The throne of God and of the Lamb shall be therein."

3. Perfect service — "And his servants shall [thus] serve him."

4. Perfect communion — "And they shall see his face" (i.e. in open vision).

5. Perfect holiness — "His Name shall be written on their foreheads" (Christ-likeness).

6. Perfect illumination — "No night"; "The Lord God giveth them light."

7. Perfect blessedness — "And they shall reign unto the ages of the ages."

What a picture! What a prospect! What a consummation! A faultless, flawless, fadeless bliss of self-fulfillment to the praise of God and of the Lamb!

Note again that the center of it all is the sovereign *throne* in which reigns the *Lamb*. He reigns there in complete oneness with God the Father, for it is "the throne of God and of the Lamb." He reigns *with* God. He reigns *for* God. He reigns *as* God. Also, he does not cease to be the Lamb! Recently I read a book in which the author (expressing what seems to be a fairly common idea) says that when our Lord, as Messiah-Sovereign, hands over the kingdom to the Father at the end of the Millennium, with all foes subjugated (1 Cor. 15:28), he thereupon ceases to be the Lamb; his manhood then disappears by absorption into his "original Godhead." I quote: "At that abdication Christ leaves His *human* glory to retire into the Divine. He ceases to rule the universe as *Man,* that He may rule it for ever and ever as God."

Surely that idea is wrong. As Hebrews 13:8 says, our Lord, by his incarnation, is now *"Jesus* Christ, the same yesterday and today and *unto the ages."* His incarnation gave him not merely a human body, but a human nature. Forevermore now he is *God-Man,* the Lion-*Lamb,* the Creator-*Redeemer;* the Sovereign-*Savior.* That is why, in the Patmos Apocalypse, the throne is said to be that of "God and the *Lamb* unto the ages of the ages." It is the tremendous, glorious, unmistakable picture of

The Lamb in absolute sovereignty forever!

Oh, the wonder of it: the divine sovereignty now and unendingly expressed through that utterly beautiful Manhood and Saviorhood! Try to think what it will mean to each of us through those "ages to come." The infinite love of the Father's boundless bosom comes to us through the incomparable tenderness of that "meek and lowly" human heart! His infinite mind will hold and surround all the millions of us who love and adore him, but (which is possible only to the infinite) he will affectionately discriminate in such a way as to love and cherish *each one of us, individually.* In that boundless ocean of immeasurable yet individualizing love there can be no food for even *adoring* jealousy among us! The song of each one of us will be, "The Son of God loved *me,* and gave himself for *me!"* (Gal. 2:20). We will sing, "My Beloved is *mine,* and I am his!" (Song 2:16). Did not his redeeming love come to us individually? Did he not save us individually? Did he not keep us individually? Has he not a plan for us individually? Then will his love ever lose sight of us individually? Never! Each one of us is uniquely precious to him. Moreover, one of the sweetest constituents of our bliss in those coming ages will be *our* sharing in his love for *others!* Thus we shall evermore discover that his joy in *all* of us is simply the aggregate of His loving joy in *each* of us.

> O Saviour mine,
> King all-divine,
> What can I say, to see Thee
> hanging there? —
> Bleeding, reviled mid vulgar
> jeer and glare;
> Lamb of Calvary!

> Oh, gladdest morn!
> Hope! hope new-born!
> Victor resplendent o'er the
> fearsome grave!
> Rising with endless, boundless
> power to save!
> Mighty Saviour!

> Now Thou dost reign,
> Jesus once slain,
> High on the sapphire, rainbow-
> circled throne!
> Thine, now, the crown and sceptre,
> Thine alone;
> King of glory!

> On that fair shore
> Myriads adore;
> Yet Thou dost deign my human
> heart to share!

Foretaste of heav'n to have Thee
reigning there:
Mine forever!

CHAPTER SIX

THE FINALITIES OF THE LAMB

---

(1) Lord and Savior

What hope we friends of Jesus share,
To whom His name is dear!
What cheer in days of anxious care,
As His return draws near!
Oh, with what longings do we burn,
His coming reign to see,
And skyward leap at His return,
With Him at last to be!

For every tear will then be dried,
And every tear be quelled,
And every yearning satisfied,
And every cloud dispelled:
And every heartache will be healed,
And every problem solved,
And every myst'ry be revealed,
And every doubt dissolved.

With deathless body, sinless mind,
Around the Saviour's throne,
Unending rapture we shall find
With Jesus and His own:
Oh, with such raptures on before,
Should we not patient be,

And love and serve Him yet the more
Until "that day" we see?

                                        — J. S. B.

THE MORE WE read the Book of Revelation, with its graphic unveilings, the more communicative it becomes if we have observant and teachable minds. Unmistakably, too, it authenticates itself as being rightly the *last* book in our Bible, for it is obviously full of divinely designed *completions*.[1] This and that and the other subject of biblical revelation all reach their completive culmination in the Patmos disclosures.

That is most of all true in the Bible doctrine of the *Lamb*. Earlier in this series we singled out and considered the main references to the Lamb in successive books of Scripture. In the Book of Revelation they reach a multiple culmination. The Lamb is actually named no less than twenty-eight times. In fact, more than anything else, the last book of the Bible is the revelation of the *Lamb*. That may well arrest us. Its meaning is bigger than words can tell.

The last book in our Bible is mainly about the *finality* of the Lamb. All else is incidental to that. All the ruling lines of Scripture doctrine reach their finality in the Lamb. Human history is to find its finality in the Lamb. All the divine purposes ultimately converge into the finality of the Lamb. Our Lord's

[1]Further comment on this is in vol. 1 of our *Explore the Book*, pp. 25-27.

lambhood is no temporary role. It has become, and will forever remain, the supremely determining factor of the universe. That is the main thrust of the Apocalypse. If we miss seeing that, we miss everything that is really vital.

Finality in the Church

In the introductory vision our risen Lord is exhibited as the final Arbiter in the *Church*. Clothed in a glory-light outshining the meridian sun he appears amid the seven golden lampstands, holding the seven stars in his hand. Of all numbers used in Holy Writ with a mystical meaning, seven appears most frequently. That is markedly so in the Book of Revelation. Usually it is to be taken representatively, which is the case in this first vision. The seven lampstands are the "seven churches" (1:20). Those seven seem meant to represent *all* the churches which in the aggregate comprise the *one* organized Church on earth.

Note that the seven are all equal. None is superior or leader to the others. They are not arranged as six around one central metropolitan lamp! There is no maternal priority of Jerusalem, or papal primacy of Rome. Those two are not even mentioned! As to organization, each of the seven is independent. Their sevenfold oneness is solely in the living Lord who moves among them, and in the soul-saving light of truth which they are meant to diffuse: a oneness of privilege and responsibility in functioning here on earth for the Lord now in heaven.

Those seven churches are a sore problem to some expositors, because in the seven letters sent to them by our Lord they seem to sustain a *legal* rather than an evangelical relationship to him. For instance, E. W. Bullinger says, "The Bible student . . . finds himself suddenly removed from the ground of *grace* to the ground of *works.*" It is said that all through, there is a doubtful "if" on the human side which seems to make salvation dependent on human works rather than on divine grace.

That mistaken view of the seven letters comes from reading them as letters to individuals instead of to *churches.* We have to see those churches as plural units. First, they are a mixture of *individuals,* with the true believers among them saved by grace alone on God's part, and by faith alone on their own part, through the atonement of Christ and regeneration by the Holy Spirit. But second, they are a membership *collectively* as a functioning unit, and although the salvation of each individual member is a matter of pure grace, the functioning of the whole assembly as a unit or "church" *cannot* be, for a corporate unit has no consciousness of its own. As individuals, the members are saved by *grace,* but the churches as collective bodies stand or fall according to their fidelity.

If a church, or "lampstand," is removed because of apostasy or other failure, its removal does not mean that it is eternally lost, for churches as corporate entities cannot be either saved or lost in that eternal sense. Only individuals are saved or lost in that sense. The removing of a church, or lampstand, is a purely *historical* rejection, and even then the "overcomers" in the dishonored church (i.e. those who remain true in doctrine and practice) still inherit the reward of faithful individuals. Moreover, in the case of those individual overcomers, although their reward is for faithful service, their eternal salvation as human souls is altogether of grace.

We do well to remember, then, that those seven churches were addressed as visible, organized units — which is why each letter begins with the singular: "I know *thy* works."

There is no shift from grace to works so far as *individuals* are concerned.

Those seven churches represent *all* such visible, organized churches, and aggregately, the *whole* visible, organized Church on earth, as distinct from that inner, *spiritual* Church composed of spiritually reborn individuals.

In each of those seven churches of long ago (just as today) there were the truly born again, as also there were others who, although *professors* of Christ, were not really *possessors* of Christ. So the seven churches are each addressed not only as collective units, but as collectively *mingled*. It is that which accounts for the phraseology of the seven letters.

Those seven churches of Revelation were *not* "Jewish assemblies," as some aver. They were all churches in Gentile cities, comprised of both Jews and Gentiles who were "all one in Christ Jesus." In that, again, they well represent the whole, outward, organized Church.

As it was in the beginning, so is it now, and shall be till this present age is over: our living Lord moves amid the lampstands; and *he* is the final Arbiter of each, of all.

Each of the seven letters begins with "I know," and ends with "I will." The "I know" indicates an all-seeing omniscience, as the penetrating diagnoses in the letters evince. The "I will" is the sign manual of royal sovereignty, of him who is "the First and the Last" (2:8), who has "the sharp two-edged sword" (2:13), and wields "authority" over "all nations" (2: 27). Each church is addressed as being accountable *directly* to that all-seeing, sovereign Lord.

It is an awe-inspiring picture: those seven lampstands diffusing their light of saving truth in a world of spiritual darkness, while hostile powers of evil strive to quench them; while at the same time, moving among those lampstands is that mysterious Figure clothed in dread splendor invisible to natural eye but awesomely vivid to evil spirit-powers. The symbolic two-edged sword which proceeds from his mouth means that he can slay his enemies with a *word*. His "eyes as a flame of fire" mean that his holiness can consume them with a *look*. His countenance, out-flashing the blaze of noonday sun, bespeaks his overwhelming power to obliterate all opposition. To demon powers, that "sword," those "eyes," that "countenance," are torture. They belong to a "Son of Man" (1:13) who met Satan on his own ground and trod the venomous serpent's head to the dust.

In his hand he *holds* "the seven stars," the "angels" or leaders of the seven churches. None can pluck them thence, which means that if they are faithful none can harm them, and if they are *un*faithful none can save them. They and the lampstands function solely for *him*. He is Son of Man and Son of God; Lamb of Calvary but Lion of Judah; boundless in grace but also absolute in wisdom, holiness, power, and sovereignty; Lord of the Church and of the churches; absolutely final in all he directs and in all he permits, whether in rewarding the praiseworthy or removing the unworthy.

Finality in Administration

The first place where our Lord is actually named the *Lamb* in the Book of Revelation is chapter 5, where in vision we see the Lamb occupy the throne of heaven. Standing out above all the incidental elements, there are three features which give that enthronement its all-eclipsing wonder.

First is the *kind* of lamb our Lord is said to be. The Greek word for a sheep is *probaton*. The word for a lamb or young sheep is *amnos*, and that is the word used of our Lord in the other New Testament passages outside the Apocalypse where

he is called the Lamb (John 1:29, 36; Acts 8:32; 1 Peter 1:
19). That is the word anyone would naturally expect. But
throughout the Book of Revelation the word is *arnion,* a diminutive which means the youngest and smallest even among
the lambs. On being told that the "Lion of the tribe of Judah"
had overcome, to open the mysterious, seven-sealed scroll,
John looked to see what would happen, but to his surprise —

> I saw in the midst of [or between] the throne
> and the four living beings, and in the midst of
> the elders, a *little lamb* standing, as though it
> had been killed (i.e. as a sacrifice) (Rev. 5:6).

John gazed and wondered at the seeming incongruity of it:
a *"little lamb"* — the meekest, gentlest, most harmless and
defenseless of all little animals, standing *there!* But the trans-
fixing surprise is to see that "little lamb" approach the throne
of the Deity, take the seven-sealed book, occupy the throne,
and assume sole authority to release the fateful contents of the
scroll into operation.

That diminutive, *arnion,* is used all through the Book of
Revelation with the same peculiar incongruity. For instance,
at the opening of the sixth seal, just before the "wrath to come"
breaks loose on the earth, we see kings, princes, rich men
and poor men calling on the rocks and mountains to fall on
them, to hide them from "the face of him that sitteth on the
throne, and from the wrath of the *little lamb"!* The vain-
glorious Lucifer once aspired to that throne of the Most High.
What an exasperating backfire on the self-exalting traitor, to
see the "little Lamb" seated there, with seraphs and elders
and angel-hosts all worshiping *him!*

But second, that "little Lamb" was "as though it had been
slain." If the expression "little Lamb" tells of our Lord's self-
humbling, his having been "slain" speaks of his *humiliation.*
There is a wide difference between self-humbling and humilia-

tion. The former is a movement from within one's own heart and mind, and is altogether voluntary, whereas humiliation is something inflicted from without, and usually against one's own will. Besides our Lord's vast and voluntary self-humbling was his *humiliation,* his being "despised and rejected," scourged, mocked, spat upon, at Satan's instigation, and then hung up in naked shame before the vulgar mob. From that fathomless humiliation on the ugly cross, the slain Lamb is lifted to the very throne of heaven, to be universally extolled as having "the Name which is above every name." Even Lucifer and his co-insurrectionists must yet cringe before that "little Lamb."

Third, and as a crowning honor, the "little Lamb" is exalted to expedite the seven-sealed divine program not as a *deputy* administrator for the Almighty, not even as the highest regent whom God could appoint, but as *co-occupant of the throne!* That is why the seraphs and elders immediately fall down "before the little Lamb" with their harps (praises) and incense vials (prayers) and render to him exactly the same worship as they do to the everlasting Father. This means that our Lord Jesus as the *Lamb* has absolute *finality of administration* throughout heaven and earth.

Finality of Saviorhood

Turn now to Revelation 7, where we see in our Lord Jesus as the Lamb a consummating finality of *Saviorhood.* Many of the visions in the Apocalypse refer exclusively to the future. Others may be called *vista* visions: they describe something going on now, but which will reach consummation in a climax yet to be. One such vista vision is that of the innumerable multitude in chapter 7.

> I saw, and behold, a great multitude which no man could number, out of every nation and of all tribes and peoples and tongues, standing before the throne and before the *Lamb,* arrayed in white robes, and having palms in their hands: and they cry with a great voice, saying: Salvation unto our God who sitteth on the throne, and unto the *Lamb.*

> And all the angels were standing round about the throne, and about the elders and the four living beings; and they fell before the throne on their faces, and worshiped God, saying: Amen; blessing and glory and wisdom and thanksgiving and honor and power be unto our God for ever and ever, Amen.

> And one of the elders answered, saying unto me: These that are arrayed in the white robes, who are they, and whence came they? And I say to him: My lord, thou knowest. And he said unto me: These are they that come out of the great tribulation, and they washed their robes and made them white in the blood of the *Lamb.* Therefore they are before the throne of God, and they serve him day and night in his temple. And he that sitteth on the throne shall spread his tabernacle over them. They shall hunger no more, neither thirst any more, nor shall the sun strike upon them, nor any heat. For the *Lamb* that is in the midst of the throne will shepherd them, and guide them to fountains

of the waters of life: and God shall wipe away every tear from their eyes" (Rev. 7:9-17).

There are those who teach that this vision refers exclusively to the end-time of the present age, to a short period of seven years (some say three-and-a-half) which they mark off as "the great tribulation." Others maintain that the words "these that come out of the great tribulation" cover the whole of the Christian dispensation. Either way, the vision depicts the ultimate bliss of our salvation in Christ.

Note the Greek present tense in verse 14: "These are they who are *coming* out of . . . ." It seems perhaps to connote a *continuity* of coming rather than one total transference from earth to heaven. In any case, John is given to see the multitude in its eventual complete immensity.

The scene is in heaven. In their countless thousands upon thousands the vast multitude are "standing before the throne and before the *Lamb.*" Here again, as in chapter 5, the classification is fourfold: "nations, tribes, peoples, tongues," the number four being, as usual, the symbolic number pertaining to the earth and the physical creation.

Those who compose that countless throng are "arrayed in *white robes*" — symbol of stainless purity. In their hands they hold "palm branches" — symbol of final victory. They unite in exulting acclamation: "Our salvation [be ascribed] to our God who sitteth on the throne, and unto the *Lamb!*" Here, as in chapter 5, the angels blend in with their sevenfold praise: "The blessing and the glory and the wisdom and the thanksgiving and the honor and the power and the might be [ascribed] to our God unto the ages of the ages."

How came those countless humans to wear those robes of now-spotless white? The answer is: "They *washed* their robes and made them white in the blood of the Lamb." That past tense refers to what they did while still on earth, and apart from which they would never have been in heaven. They were now in heaven through the blood. That is why verse 15 says, "Therefore are they before the throne of God. . . ." Their absolute cleansing from the guilt and stain of sin they owe utterly to the *Lamb*. In the vision of chapter 5 the praise was for our having been *"purchased"* by the blood. Here, in chapter 7, it is for our having been *"purified"* by the blood. In 12:11, we see the overcomers *"prevailing"* through the blood. Oh, the wonder of that "precious blood"!

But now see the further *felicity* of that raptured multitude. Not only are they "before the throne of God," bathed in its ineffable glory-light, but they "serve him day and night" in his heavenly "sanctuary," which means that their blissful state is augmented by the serene joy of sinless ministry. Furthermore, "He that sitteth on the throne shall spread his tabernacle over them," pavilioning them in unending tranquility and security and overspreading them as the Shekinah (symbol of the divine Presence) covered the Mercy Seat with its gentle splendor long ago. And again: "They shall *not* [emphatic] hunger any more, *not* thirst any more; the sun shall *not* strike on them; no, nor any heat" — phraseology which blends both the literal and the symbolic to indicate that every need, physical, mental, spiritual, and all worthy desire, is forever satisfied, with nothing ever to cause weakness or fatigue.

Do we ask *how* all this is theirs? Verse 17 answers: "For [i.e. because] the *Lamb* in the midst of the throne shall *shepherd* them. . . ." So he is both Lamb and Shepherd! That is no mixing of metaphors: it is a union of precious realities in the one manifold Savior. That which *opens* heaven to us is the blood of the Calvary *Lamb*. That which *makes* heaven for us is the love of that divine-human *Shepherd*. And he leads us to "springs of living waters," which means unending renewal in a life of rapturous purity and buoyant energy.

The concluding word is: "And God shall wipe away every tear from their eyes," which implies that every *cause* of tears is forever obliterated: no more pain, fear, regret, persecution, privation, misunderstanding, temptation, failure, weakness, martyrdom, imprisonment, poverty, hunger, sickness, death, bereavement. Every pain and pang and imperfection will be gone, even the memory of them becoming lost in ages of unfolding compensations.

This, then, is the tenfold picture of final salvation in that uncountable host of saved sinners now transplanted to heaven as the glorified saints.

1. "Before the throne" — beatific vision
2. "White robes" — unsullied holiness
3. "Palm branches" — finalized victory
4. "They serve him" — highest ministry
5. "He covers them" — unending security
6. "Hunger no more" — fulfillment for ever
7. "Sun smites not" — felicity without flaw
8. "He shepherds them" — serenity in his love
9. "Living waters" — ageless immortality
10. "Every tear" dried — joy, perfect, fadeless.

Amid our present limitations of mortal flesh and impaired mental faculties, even when we enjoy most vigorous health of body and keenest agility of mind, we simply cannot imagine realistically what it will be to experience that life of utter ecstasy yonder. With sinless hearts, and with minds continuously penetrated by direct rays of holy radiance from that dearest face in the universe; with perfected powers and expanded capacities of thought and worship and love and service; surrounded by lofty opportunities and incentives and amplitudes such as we have never known before; all that, amid the unclouded, open vision of *his smile*: what must it be!

We are not being sentimentally impractical when we long for such a bliss as *that!* On the contrary, we are strangely calloused and spiritually phlegmatic if we do not! To let our minds linger gratefully on that coming glory, other than turn-

ing us into inactive visionaries, animates us with one of the
healthiest stimulants of the Christian faith.

> Artistic Spring awakes the flowers,
>   And paints the landscape fair,
> But Autumn wilts the gayest bowers,
>   And Winter strips them bare.
> Oh, for the land of light and love
>   Free from all blight and gloom!
> Oh, for that Paradise above,
>   Where flowers unfading bloom!
>
> The questing eye and supple limb
>   Of youth's romantic hour,
> How swiftly gone! Its vigours dim
>   In quickly jaded power:
> Oh, for the life of ageless day,
>   Mounting on eagle's wings!
> Oh, for the youth beyond decay,
>   To serve my King of Kings!
>
> How oft on earth the spirit faints
>   And mourns o'er inward sin!
> But yonder the enraptured saints
>   Know sinless bliss within!
> Oh, for a deeper faith and prayer!
>   Stir us, dear Lord divine;
> Seal us and guard us till we share
>   That bliss with Thee and Thine.

It is years since I wrote the above three verses, to be used
as a hymn in connection with a sermon of mine. I was still a
young man. I can recall the feelings, the longings, which
prompted my pen to write away back then, during a season of
busy and very tiring activity in Christian work. Were those

lines a product of dreamy listlessness? Did those longings cause my hands to drop into pious inactivity or luxurious uselessness? The very opposite! Always my thoughts of what awaits us yonder have nerved me afresh to persevere in earnest Christian endeavor amid the ugly sin and poignant need everywhere around us.

But take another look at that "multitude which no man could number" there in that "excellent glory." How came they there? Every one of that numberless throng came there "through the blood of the *Lamb*" (v. 14). Where do they gather and exult? "Before the throne and before the *Lamb*" (v. 9). What is their heaven of joy? It is this: "The *Lamb* in the midst of the throne shall shepherd them" (v. 17). It is a surpassingly wonderful photograph of final glorification, and it all centers in *the finality of the Lamb as our Savior*. He is the sweetness, the fullness, and the everlasting finality of it all. Well may we sing with C. E. Mudie,

> To Thee, dear Calvary Lamb,
>   I all things owe:
> All that I have and am,
>   And all I know.
> All that I have is now
>   no longer mine,
> And I am not my own,
>   Lord, I am Thine.
>
> How can I, Lord, withhold
>   Life's brightest hour
> From Thee, or gathered gold,
>   Or any power?
> How can I keep one precious
>   thing from Thee,
> When Thou hast giv'n Thine own
>   dear Self for me?

I pray Thee, Saviour, keep
  Me in Thy love,
Until death's holy sleep
  Shall me remove
To that fair realm where,
      sin and sorrow o'er,
Thou and Thine own are one
    for evermore.

CHAPTER SEVEN

THE FINALITIES OF THE LAMB

(2) Judge and King

Kingdoms and empires, age by age,
File quickly by on history's page;
Vaunting in conquest, one by one,
They waxed a season, and were gone:
Lord of the Church, whom we adore,
Thy crown alone lasts evermore.

Strangely and swiftly in our day
Historic thrones have passed away;
Earth-girdling new philosophies
Spread vast, collective tyrannies:
Lord of the Church, again appear,
Thy reign of truth establish here.

Despots, inflated, scorn Thy crown;
Thy iron rod shall smite them down;
Satan to Hades shall be hurled,
Thy worldwide banner be unfurled:
Lord of the Church, return, we pray;
Bring in Thy warless, global sway.

No weapon men may yet employ
Can ever Thy dear Church destroy;

No nuclear missile man invents
Can breach its lofty battlements:
Lord of the Church, no more refrain;
The time is ripe: return and reign!

— J. S. B.

LET US CONTINUE our reflections on the finalities of our Lord as the Lamb. It is a subject flashing with brilliant and varied facets. Some of its gladder implications we have reviewed, though all too inadequately, and our hearts have already blended in chorus with that raptured multitude on high as they sing, "Glory to the Lamb!"

Finality in Retribution

But there are aspects in the finalities of the Lamb which may well be frightening to the ungodly. He is the Executive of the divine *wrath,* particularly of the age-end "wrath to come" — that concentrated few years of catastrophe with which the present dispensation is to close. That cloudburst of terminal wrath is plainly foretold in various Scriptures, and startlingly depicted in some of the Apocalyptic visions. Its breaking forth is seen when the Lamb unlooses the sixth seal of the seven-sealed scroll.

> And I saw when he opened the sixth seal, and
> there was a great earthquake; the sun became
> black as sackcloth of hair, and the whole moon
> became as blood: and the stars of heaven fell
> unto the earth, as a fig tree casteth her unripe
> figs when she is shaken of a great wind. And
> the heaven was removed as a scroll when it is
> rolled up; and every mountain and island were
> moved out of their places. And the kings of the
> earth, and the princes, and the chief captains,
> and the rich and the strong and every bondman
> and freeman, hid themselves in the caves and
> in the rocks of the mountains: and they say to
> the mountains and the rocks: Fall on us, and
> hide us from the face of him that sitteth on the
> throne, and from *the wrath of the Lamb;* for
> the great day of their wrath is come; and who is
> able to stand? (Rev. 6:12-17).

I would not presume to speak with any dogmatism on this
point, but it seems to me that Scripture makes a distinction
which is usually disregarded. I mean a distinction between
the "great tribulation" and the "wrath to come." Our Lord
makes that distinction in his Olivet forecast in Matthew 24.
In verses 21 to 28 he certainly speaks of the "great tribulation," telling us that it will be "such as hath not been from the
beginning of the world," but at verse 29 he makes a sharp
time distinction, saying, "Immediately *after* the 'tribulation' of
those days, the sun shall be darkened, and the moon shall not
give her light, and the stars shall fall from heaven, and the
powers of the heavens shall be shaken: and then shall appear
the sign of the Son of Man in heaven; and then shall all the
tribes of the earth mourn. . . ."

That same distinction between the "great tribulation" and
the "wrath of God" is marked by that sixth seal in Revelation

6. Up to that point there certainly has been "tribulation" (see verses 3 to 11), but now "the great day of the *wrath* is reached" (vv. 16, 17). Indeed, there is a parallel between our Lord's Olivet predelineation and those seven seals of the Apocalypse which is too pronounced and significant to be overlooked.

Matthew 24	*Revelation 6*
"Many shall come in my name, saying, I am the Christ, and shall lead many astray" (v. 5).	First seal. "A *white* horse; and he that sat thereon had a bow . . . and he came forth conquering and to conquer" (v. 2).
"Wars and rumors of wars . . . for these must needs come to pass . . . nation against nation and kingdom against kingdom" (vv. 6, 7).	Second seal. "A *red* horse; and to him that sat thereon it was given to take peace from the earth, that they should slay one another" (v. 4).
"And there shall be famines . . . in various places" (v. 7).	Third seal. "A *black* horse; and he that sat thereon had a balance . . . A measure of wheat for a shilling . . . hurt not the oil and wine" (vv. 5, 6).
"And earthquakes in various places . . . All these are the beginning of travail" (vv. 7, 8).	Fourth seal. "A *pale* horse; and he that sat upon him, his name was Death; and Hades followed him" (v. 8).
"They shall deliver you to tribulation, and kill you; and ye shall be hated of all nations for my Name's sake" (v. 9; amplified in verses 15-28).	Fifth seal. "I saw underneath the altar the souls of them that had been slain for the Word of God, and for the testimony which they held" (vv. 9, 10).
"Immediately *after* the tribulation of those days the sun shall be darkened, and the moon shall not give her light, and the stars shall fall from heaven and the powers of the heavens shall be shaken: and then shall appear the sign of the Son of Man in heaven: and then shall all the tribes of the earth mourn:	Sixth seal. "There was a great earthquake; and the sun became black as sackcloth of hair, and the whole moon became as blood: the stars of the heaven fell unto the earth . . . and the heaven was removed as a scroll . . . And the kings of the earth, and the princes . . . bondman and freeman hid themselves

Matthew 24 (continued)

and they shall see the Son of Man coming on the clouds of heaven with power and great glory" (vv. 29, 30).

"And he shall send forth his *angels* with a great sound of a trumpet, and they shall gather together his *elect* from the four winds, from one end of heaven to the other" (v. 31).

Revelation 6 (continued)

. . . and say to the mountains and rocks: Fall on us and hide us from the face of him that sitteth on the throne and from the wrath of the Lamb" (vv. 12-16).

Seventh seal. First the 144,000 *elect* sealed on earth (7:4-8) and "multitude" in heaven (vv. 9-17), then the seventh seal — "seven *angels*" with the "seven *trumpets*" of the now-beginning "wrath" (8:1).

So, then, that sixth seal brings us to the point when (with the *seventh* seal) the "wrath to come" breaks forth. Up to that point it has been the "great tribulation," but that now runs into the "wrath of God." The "great tribulation" is something caused by man — especially by "the man of sin," the culminating embodiment of Antichrist, the "beast" whose cryptic number is 666; whereas the "wrath to come" is something inflicted by *God* — even "the wrath of the Lamb." The seven unloosed seals bring us right *to* that epoch of "wrath." The seven "trumpets" and seven "bowls" which follow show us what will happen *in* it. My own reading of the Apocalypse along with other Scriptures convinces me that this "wrath to come" covers the last three-and-a-half years of the present age.

We are often asked, "Will the Church go through the great tribulation?" The question itself is out of focus. How *can* the Church go through that future period here on earth when the vast majority of those who compose the Church are already in heaven and will remain there until our Lord's visible return to this planet? The real question at issue is: Will there be Christian believers on earth at that time? Overdogmatism as to that has too often been unloving, and damaging to our Lord's work through his people. To my own mind it seems wiser at present to be tentative rather than headstrong on that point. My own persuasion is that there *will* be Christian believers on earth then, though I am open for further guidance.

This, however, is certain, that whenever God allows his Shadrachs, Meshachs and Abed-negos to go through the seven-times heated furnace there is always One "like the Son of God" who walks with them in it. If we had asked those three worthies about their ordeal afterward, they would have said, "We wouldn't have missed it for anything." In line with that, as I now look back, I can see in my own experience that my larger discoveries of the heavenly Presence with me have come in times of trial or stress. Those, I agree, are comparatively minor considerations belonging to just one individual, but they are reassuring to *me,* and I am content to let the matter rest there. Whatever may or may not immediately precede the sudden "shout" of the descending heavenly Bridegroom, I want to be ready for *that!* I would not needlessly *provoke* either tribulation or martyrdom — but I fain would have the Shadrach, Meshach and Abed-nego *spirit!*

What a picture of consternation that sixth seal releases! See who they are who call on the rocks and mountains to fall on them. They are "kings, nobles, military commanders, the rich, the strong, the bondman, the freeman." The first six categories are men of power, courage, daring — not easily terrified, but used to scenes of conflict or challenge. At the other extreme, "bondmen" are usually least alarmed, for they have least to lose. But here is something which terrifies *all* kinds of men.

What is it? Well, for one thing, there is the greatest earthquake in history. Of all the freak phenomena of nature, none excites such frenzy, distraction, stark terror as a major earthquake. Whatever other catastrophe may overtake us, so long as the ground beneath us remains firm — the "solid earth" as we call it — there is at least a sense of basic stability. But when the earth itself reels and rolls, rocks and cracks, there is absolutely no hiding place, nowhere to run. Our whole system of thinking and reasoning loses its equilibrium. Not only humans, but the lower animals also, give way to strangest panic.

Until recently many orthodox expositors have held that the sun's becoming as black sackcloth, and the moon as blood, and stars falling to the earth, must be taken as purely visional symbols, not as actual disturbances of the elements. But present-day happenings, discoveries, unprecedented weapons of vast destruction, and predictable likelihoods in nature itself, may well make us revise our thinking. If *such* an earthquake, with such hitherto unknown accompaniments, seems unthinkable because unprecedented, we should reflect that this *coming* upheaval is by sovereign intention to *exceed* all former earthquakes. It is to be the most fearful ever.

Furthermore, in the correspondence which we have noted between Matthew 24 and Revelation 6, our Lord's Olivet words which parallel this sixth seal certainly do foretell, not in symbol but with obviously intended literalness, unprecedented and frightening abnormalities in the heavenly bodies. "Immediately after the tribulation of those days the sun shall be darkened, and the moon shall not give her light, and the stars shall fall from heaven, and the powers of the heavens shall be shaken." The wording is neither rhetorical nor hyperbolic. It is the language of phenomenal *appearance,* and as such is accurate and unexaggerated. The content of that sixth seal will thus be terrifyingly actual.

That, however, is not the only cause of the frantic alarm. Amid those bewildering cosmic terrors the godless and the wicked of the earth see *Someone* right in the center — as if the moon were suddenly to swing so near to the earth as to fill the sky and seem about to smother us all. Instinctively they know who it is, and they cry out, "Hide us from the face of the Sitter on the throne and from the wrath of the *Lamb;* for the great day of their wrath is come, and who is able to stand?" What they now see is, as Paul expresses it, the overpowering "glory of God *in the face of Jesus Christ"* (2 Cor. 4:6).

That which makes their remorse and sickening dread the more torturing is that the inescapable retribution is "the wrath of the *Lamb*" — the unanswerable vengeance of the "meek and lowly" Jesus whom they have "despised and rejected," the One whose redeeming love and atoning blood they have "trodden underfoot" like some "unholy thing" (Heb. 10:29). *His* wrath carries a condemnation from which there is no escape, for besides being condemned of God they are now uselessly *self*-condemned.

The "wrath of the *Lamb*"! Wrath is not mere temper; temper is always irrational, emotion gone berserk; therefore temper is *never* right. Nor is wrath some savage personal revenge. Wrath is righteous anger executing vengeance against wickedness. Righteous wrath is an awesome thing. The wrath of a noble father whose long-suffering forgiveness has been outraged is far more awesome than the temper of a tyrant. The eventual wrath of mocked love is far more terrible than hate. It is "the wrath of the *Lamb*" (the "little Lamb"!) which is so crushing. Whoever saw a lamb in a rage? A lion, a tiger, or any other tantalized beast, yes; but the "wrath of the *Lamb*" . . . ! The degree to which wrath is terrible is determined by three factors: (1) whose it is, (2) the reason for it, (3) the form it takes. Let those three together tell us why the wrath of the Lamb is so prostrating.

That sixth seal, then, marks the transition from the "great tribulation" to the "wrath of God"; for with the opening of the *seventh* seal the seven *trumpets* of that sevenfold wrath begin to sound, one after the other. During the "great tribulation" history's culminating Antichrist, namely, the "beast," the "man of sin" whose number is 666, has had things *his* way, raging against Israel and all who hold "the testimony of Jesus." But now "wrath from heaven" is rained down on *him,* along with all his accomplices and followers. The seventh seal brings us to that last three-and-a-half years, or forty-two months (Rev. 11:2; 12:5), or 1260 days (Rev. 11:3; 12:6), or "time and times and half a time" (Rev. 12:14), or the second half of the seventieth week (Dan. 9:27) when "wrath shall be poured out upon the desolator." (See especially E.R.V. or R.S.V.)

It is at once arresting that between the sixth and seventh seals the 144,000 of *Israel* are sealed on earth for preservation through the coming wrath period (7:1-8), and then the countless multitude of the saved from *"every* nation" is seen in heaven singing "salvation to our God." We are meant to see thereby God's preservation of his elect both through and from the "great tribulation" and the "wrath" which follows it. Then there is a solemn pause, or suspenseful silence (8:1) before the seven trumpets of the wrath begin sounding (Rev. 8:6).

Observant readers will have noticed that from the first trumpet (8:6) to the seventh (11:15) we are *inside* that final three-and-a-half years of concentrated intensity (compare 9:11 with 11:7 and references to the forty-two months). Chapters 12 to 14 confirm that the "dragon" and the "beast" and the "false prophet" are all here together on earth *at that time.* Then, as if to give us decisive confirmation, we are shown the seven angels with the seven bowls containing the seven plagues in which is *"finished* the wrath of God" (15:1).

The parallel between those seven bowls and the preceding seven trumpets is too clear to be doubted, and it confirms (at least to my own mind) that the period is one and the same. Both the trumpets and the bowls are coterminus, i.e. they end at Armageddon and the actual coming of the Messianic kingdom. If the trumpets and bowls are not the same "wrath" period, then the bowls are surely the final intensification of it.

The Seven Trumpets		*The Seven Bowls*
First:	On the earth (8:7).	On the earth (16:2).
Second:	On the sea (8:8).	On the sea (16:3).
Third:	On the rivers (8:10).	On the rivers (16:4).
Fourth:	Sun, moon (8:12).	On the sun (16:8).
Fifth:	Men smitten (9:1-11).	Men smitten (16:10).

Sixth:	Euphrates (9:13-21).	Euphrates (16:12-16).
Seventh:	Divine wrath on "nations" (11:17, 18). "Thunders and earthquake" (11:19). World becomes kingdom of Christ (11:15-17).	"It [wrath] is done" (16:17). "Cities of nations" fall (16:19). "Thunders . . . great earthquake" (16:18). Babylon destroyed and Christ comes as King of Kings (17:1—19:21).

Any reader who takes time to compare the related passages soon sees that the whole variegated movement converges on Armageddon (or Har-Megiddo, or Har-Magedon, i.e., Mount Megiddo) where the *Lamb,* now spectacularly descending to earth as *KING OF KINGS AND LORD OF LORDS,* forever obliterates the alliance of the dragon and the beast and the false prophet, tramples underfoot all opposition, and brings in his global reign. This the following three passages show in parallel.

Revelation 16:12 etc.	*Revelation 17:12-14*	*Revelation 19:11-16*
And the sixth angel poured out his bowl on the great river Euphrates; and the water thereof was dried up, that the way might be made ready for the kings that come from the sunrising. And I saw coming out of the mouth of the dragon . . . three unclean spirits . . . which go forth unto the kings . . . to gather them unto the war of the great day of God, the Almighty. . . . And they gathered them together into the place which is called in Hebrew Har-Magedon.	The ten horns . . . are ten kings who have received no kingdom as yet; but they receive authority as kings, with the beast, for one hour. These have one mind, and they give their power and authority unto the beast. These shall war against the *Lamb,* and the *Lamb* shall overcome them; for he is Lord of lords and King of kings. And they also shall overcome that are with him, called and chosen and faithful.	I saw heaven opened; and behold, a white horse, and he that sat thereon, called Faithful and True: and in righteousness he doth judge and make war. His eyes are a flame of fire, and upon his head are many diadems. . . . And the armies which are in heaven followed him on white horses . . . Out of his mouth proceedeth a sharp sword, that with it he should smite the nations. . . . He treadeth the winepress of the wrath of God. And he hath . . . a name written: *KING OF KINGS AND LORD OF LORDS.*

Armageddon culminates and exhausts the fearful but fully deserved vengeance of God. With that "wrath of the Lamb" the account is settled, the "controversy of Jehovah" is over, the vengeance of Heaven is completed. In this final judgment we are given to see that the Lamb who has absolute finality as the race's Sinbearer and heavenly Administrator, has also an absolute finality as the *Executor of the divine wrath.*

I believe that this world-staggering "wrath to come" is now near. The stage is being set for that last grim week of years in which the features of the beast (666) and the false prophet and the harlot will have become recognized beyond mistake by those who know the written Word of God. All eyes today may well be on the Middle East, which will be the *center* of that final act in the six-thousand-year drama, as it will also involve all the major nations of our time.

Finality of Rule

Despite all appearances to the contrary, this world of ours belongs to the *Lamb.* It is his as God the Son, by creative right. It is his as the Son of Abraham and David, by messianic title. Crowningly it is his as the Lamb, by redemptive purchase. It is also to be his by military conquest, as various prophecies foretell and the Book of Revelation fore-pictures. It will also be his (I speak reverently) by popular vote. Ask the millions and millions of the saved now in heaven (who will return to earth with him) whom *they* want as king (Rev. 7: 9). Ask the whole realm of created beings in heaven and on earth (5:13). Ask all the sealed of Israel (14:1-5), and the regathered millions of the earthly Israel after they "look on him whom they pierced," and recognize him (Zech. 12:10). Ask all the "meek of the earth" (Isa. 11:14; Matt. 5:5).

There will be depraved leaders and hordes of Gog who will hate and oppose, but they shall be crumpled into mute impotency, smitten with a sword of fire and ruled with a rod of iron. Yes, for the first thing which our holy Lord will do, upon his lightning re-entry from the outer spaces, is to "make war" (Rev. 19:11). That, at long last, will indeed be "the war to *end* war." It will be sudden and final. After that overwhelming conquest he will reign as "King of Peace" in Salem. After that demolishing blaze of wrath he will rule all the nations (Rev. 12:5; 20:4-6).

Once again the seeming incongruity becomes conspicuous; i.e., the titanic smashup of all evil powers on this earth is to be inflicted by the flaming fury of "the little Lamb," who is now seen as *"KING OF KINGS AND LORD OF LORDS"!*

> After these things I heard as it were a great voice of a great multitude in heaven, saying: Hallelujah; salvation and glory and power belong to our God. True and righteous are his judgments; for he hath judged the great harlot, her that corrupted the earth with her fornication; and he hath avenged the blood of his servants at her hand.
>
> And a second time they say, Hallelujah. And her smoke goeth up for ever and ever. And the four and twenty elders and the four living ones [the seraphs] fell down and worshipped God who sitteth on the throne, saying, Amen; Hallelujah. . . . Hallelujah: for the Lord our God, the Almighty reigneth. Let us rejoice and be exceeding glad, and let us give the glory unto him; for the *marriage of the Lamb* is come, and

> his wife hath made herself ready. And it was
> given unto her that she should array herself in
> fine linen, bright and pure: for the fine linen is
> the righteous acts of the saints. And he saith
> unto me: Write, Blessed are they that are bid-
> den to the *marriage supper of the Lamb* (Rev.
> 19:1-9).

This is the goal of all biblical prophecy: the return and reign of Christ. After the "wrath of the Lamb" comes the "marriage of the Lamb." The bride, as seems clear from the paragraph here quoted and from other references, is the transformed and transfigured city of Jerusalem: not that city, of course, merely as a city of magnificent architecture and incomparable elegance, but Jerusalem as mystically representing our Lord's own blood-bought people, who now enter and share with him his millennial rule and endless reign. Indeed, the bride is plainly identified in Rev. 19:8 as "the *saints,*" those already described in 17:14 as "chosen and called and faithful."

That city is the inheritance of *all* our Lord's "saints" — those of the true, spiritual Church completed and raptured at his return, and then on earth again in their immortalized bodies — together with all those of the earthly Israel — a nation which, by a nation-wide spiritual eye-opening, will have become a restored, regenerated people (in fulfillment of such promises as Jeremiah 31:29-36; Ezekiel 37:21-26) recognizing and adoring Jesus, at last, as Messiah-Savior (Zechariah 12:10 and 14:9, 20). New York, London, Moscow, Peking, Tokyo, Berlin, Paris — all will be eclipsed. There will be supernatural splendors about Jerusalem then which no other city has ever known, and the King of Kings himself will reign there in a visible presence radiating supernal light throughout the whole city. "Every eye shall see him" (Rev.

1:7), continuously around the whole world, by ubiquitous television, and all the earth's peoples will hear that wonderful voice "as the sound of many waters" speaking to them directly from Jerusalem, for "out of Zion shall go forth the law, and the word of Jehovah from Jerusalem" (Isa. 2:3).

Jerusalem will be the legislative and governmental center of the globe. It will be acknowledged as such by all nations. It will be a magnetic center where heavenly glory will be made visible to the eyes of men. Zion will be the citadel of omnipotence which allows not a breath of insurrection, and tolerates no breach of commercial honesty anywhere on earth. From there the eyes of omniscience will continually survey all people, with benign comfort to the upright but deterrent warning to would-be evil-doers.

A world-girdling Christocracy will be here, demonstrating our Lord's absolute finality of rule as the *Lamb*. That rule of warless tranquility and unparalleled scientific progress, having crushed out the last vestige of earthly anti-Godism, will merge into the postmillennial reign of the Lamb through timeless aeons. In the Book of Revelation there are certain phrases which are so recurrent as to be characteristic. One of these is the Greek *eis tous aionas tōn aionōn*: "to the ages of the ages." It occurs thirteen times — more than all other New Testament occurrences. So far as I know, the Greek language did not have any single word which expressed absolute eternity. It used the nearest possible phrase: "to the ages of the ages," meaning boundless perpetuity. That is the phrase used of our Lord's reign as the *Lamb*. See Revelation 11:15.

> The world-kingdom of our Lord and of his Christ
> is come; and he shall reign unto the ages of the
> ages.

Finality in Judgment

In all the Bible there is not a more solemn paragraph than Revelation 20:11-15. It pictures the final, general judgment of human beings at the throne of God. Clearly this judgment is after the Millennium. The wording indicates that it is racial and that it settles individual destiny for ever. That judgment also marks the dissolution of the present cosmic system, for death (of the body) and hades (present detention-place of the disembodied departed) are forever done away, and a new order ensues.

> I saw a great white throne, and him that sat on it, from whose face the earth and the heaven fled away, and there was found no place for them. And I saw the dead, the great and the small, standing before the throne: and the books were opened; and another book was opened which is the book of life. And the dead were judged out of the things which were written in the books, according to their works. And the sea gave up the dead that were in it: and death and hades gave up the dead that were in them: and they were judged, every man, according to their works. And death and hades were cast into the lake of fire. This is the second death, even the lake of fire. And if any was not found written in the book of life, he was cast into the lake of fire (Rev. 20:11-15).

The basis of the judgment is: "according to their works." So no man will perish for Adam's sin, i.e., for an inherited depravity which he could not escape. The One who sits on that throne is the omniscient Psychologist. His diagnoses are as infallible as his righteousness is inflexible and his verdicts inexorable. The blood of the *Lamb,* the atonement of Christ, covers all hereditary evil which we human beings involuntarily inherit in Adam. The sentence will correspond with exquisite exactness to individual responsibility. But that which is absolutely determinative is:

> And another book was opened, which is *the book of life.* . . . And if any was not found written in the book of life, he was cast into the lake of fire.

The *"book of life."* Whose is it? Who decides the entries and deletions? The Apocalypse leaves us in no doubt. In 13: 8 and again in 21:27 that book is called "the *Lamb's* book of life." His also is the hand which inscribes or excludes according to his own sovereign decision, for in 3:5 he says, "He that overcometh shall be arrayed in white raiment, and I will in no wise *blot his name out of* the book of life." Oh, the power of that nail-pierced hand! Oh, the tremendous meaning of the *Lamb!* The final judging and ultimate destiny of all humans are *his!*

Finality of Deity

At the present time a subtle and deceiving distinction is being drawn by certain movements and writers between our Lord's divinity and his intrinsic deity. Formerly, when our

Savior's "divinity" was referred to, it was understood to mean his co-equality and eternality with the Father. For instance, Canon H. P. Liddon's classic book *The Divinity of our Lord* is a masterly survey of Scripture witness to our Lord's eternal Godhead. But today, the word "divinity" as used of him often means something less — *infinitely* less, for the difference between the Creator and *any* created being is infinite.

As already noted, the Apocalypse fittingly comes last in our Bible because of its completive additions to recurrent topics of scriptural revelation. Another instance of that completive function is its testimony to our Lord's true *deity*. Indeed, there is no part of Scripture which exhibits so repeatedly, side by side, our Lord's personal *distinction* from the Father and yet his indivisible *oneness* with the Father.

The following are instances of his being personally *distinguished* from the Father: Revelation 1:1 and 6; 3:2, 12, 21; 5:7 and 13; 6:16 and 17; 7:10 and 17; 11:15; 12:10 and 17; 14:1, 4, 12; 19:14. But traveling along with those, all the way through, there are the most definite implications of his co-equal identification in Godhead with the Father. We cannot here refer to them all, but we point out a few examples. We turn first to chapter 1, verses 7 and 8.

> Behold, he cometh with the clouds; and every eye shall see him, and they that pierced him; and all the tribes of the earth shall mourn over him. Even so. Amen. I am the Alpha and the Omega, saith the Lord God, who is, and who was, and who is to come; the Almighty.

The natural thing is to take the words, "I am the Alpha and the Omega. . . . The Almighty," as spoken by our Lord Jesus of himself, as his signature to the preceding statement, "Behold, he cometh with the clouds. . . ." That is the more in keeping because of the twice occurring word, "cometh," i.e., "Behold he *cometh*. . . . I am Alpha and Omega, who is, and who was, and who *cometh*."

However, there are those who insist that the words of verse 8 are spoken by God the Father, that he alone is the eternal "Alpha and Omega," the "Almighty." They strengthen their case by reference to verse 4: "Grace to you, and peace, from him who is and who was and who is to come; and from the seven spirits which are before his throne, *and* [as distinct from the Almighty] from Jesus Christ. . . ."

Yet all must agree that just afterward, in verse 18, it is our Lord Jesus who speaks: "I am the First and the Last [i.e. Alpha and Omega], the living One; and I became dead; and behold, I am alive unto the ages of the ages." Moreover, lest even a shadow of doubt should linger in any reader's mind, the Book of Revelation settles the matter once for all in its closing paragraph. See 22:12 and following. It is our Lord Jesus speaking: "Behold, I come quickly, and my reward is with me, to render to each man according to his work. *I am the Alpha and the Omega,* the First and the Last, the Beginning and the End. . . . I, Jesus, have sent mine angel to testify unto you these things."

So there it is: the very phraseology which applies exclusively to absolute Deity is used of and by our Lord Jesus. Equally with the Father, he is the uncreated Alpha and Omega. In the most conclusive way it evinces his essential identity of being with the eternal Father. Utter marvel: the *Lamb* is none other than *God!*

Turning now to chapters 4 and 5, we find this same mystery of the Godhead expressed in another way. John sees the flashing, rainbow-circled "throne set in heaven," with the seven flambeaux burning before it, and the four flame-like seraphs encompassing it, uttering their continuous antiphony, "Holy . . . holy . . . holy is the Lord God, the Almighty." Round about that central throne he sees the four-and-twenty subsidiary thrones occupied by the twenty-four white-robed "elders." Then amid the lightnings and thunders emanating from the throne, he hears the worship.

> Worthy art thou, our Lord and our God, to re-
> ceive the glory and the honor and the power;
> for thou didst create all things; and because of
> thy will they are, and were created (4:11).

The vision moves on to its climactic surprise — "the *Lamb*"*!* That "little Lamb" — slain yet living — approaches that throne of the "Almighty" and occupies it, and does so with a propriety at once acknowledged by all the heavenly observers, for the guardian seraphs and royal elders now "fall down before the *Lamb*," with harp-chords of praise and incense-odors of prayer and prostrate worship, while the vast outer ring of angel myriads blends with them in ascribing to the *Lamb* the very same "glory" and "honor" and "power" which they ascribe (chapter 4) to the "Almighty." In other words, the Lamb is equally and inseparably one with the Father as the object of creature *worship*.

Strange as it seems, there are movements and writers today who call themselves Christian yet are bent on *denying* that enthronement of the Lamb. Seizing on triviality (as it seems to me) they ask how the Lamb could be at one and the same time both "in the midst of the throne" and yet "in the midst" of the elders. They would translate the Greek word to mean that the Lamb was "between" the throne and the elders. They also point to the end of the chapter, where *all* creatures sing: "Unto him that sitteth on the throne, *and* unto the Lamb. . . ." — which is supposed to differentiate between the one and only "Almighty" who alone sits on the throne, and the Lamb who is only *before* it. But they misplead the Scripture. The four seraphs and twenty-four elders are themselves all ranged *"round* the throne" (4:4, 6). To be "in the midst" of *them* is to be "in the midst" of *it,* the throne. Nor is that all, for our dear Lord himself says, "Even as I overcame, and sat down *with my Father in his throne*" (3:21).

Is even that not enough to convince the doubter? Then the Book of Revelation will settle it for us conclusively in its closing vision where, in its last reference to that throne of the universe, it twice names it "the throne of God *and* of the *Lamb*" (22:1, 3). Yes, the Lamb is in that throne as being one in absolute *Deity* with the Father.

We might usefully linger over several other passages in the Apocalypse where the deity of the Lamb is similarly denoted, but we mention only one more. It comes in the last and most sublime of the Patmos unveilings. John is privileged to see the New Jerusalem in the coming "new heaven and new earth." It is a city of such surpassing splendor and beauty, filled with such delectable conditions, as earth has never known before. It blends the heavenly with the earthly, and the celestial with the terrestrial. In a way never known before, it is "heaven on earth."

But amid its pearly gates and jasper walls and golden streets and ivory palaces, there was something missing as John's ravished gaze lingered over it, something which John expected would be the center of everything, and for which he apparently looked particularly. There was no temple or sanctuary! Then he perceived the reason. No temple was needed, for God himself was actually there in visible presence, and therefore not needing to be either represented or approached by means of any emblematical building. In visible shekinah God is seen and worshiped there!

How significant is the way John describes it! "A temple I saw not in it; for the Lord God, the Almighty, is its temple, *and so is the Lamb*." Similarly, as the Father and the Son are together the temple, so are they together the *light*: "The city hath no need of the sun, nor of the moon, that they should shine on it, for the glory of God lighted it, *and its luminary is the Lamb*."

Mystery of mysteries: when we see the Lamb we are seeing God! God is not only the "Almighty." No, in his ineffably glorious, eternal Son, he is also the Lamb-Redeemer! Let all worlds wonder, and all creatures adore! As we have seen, our Lord Jesus as the Lamb is co-equally one with the eternal Father by identical designation as "the Alpha and the Omega" (1:8 with 22:12), then by joint-enthronement in heaven (5: 8-14), then by oneness with the Father as the temple and the light and the King and the glorious God *worshiped* in the New Jerusalem (21 and 22).

Well may we wonder and worship as we reflect upon those seven finalities of the Lamb exhibited to us in that last book of the Bible: (1) finality as Lord of the Church, (2) finality as universal Administrator, (3) finality as Savior-Shepherd of his people, (4) finality in age-end retribution, (5) finality of ruling power, (6) finality as Judge of all, (7) finality of absolute Godhead. What a climax of revelation! What a Savior! What a God! Glory to the Lamb!

> Thou art the everlasting Word,
>   The uncreated Son;
> God manifestly seen and heard,
>   And Heaven's beloved One:
> Worthy, O Lamb of God, art Thou
> That every knee to Thee should bow.
>
> In Thee most perfectly expressed
>   The Father's glories shine;
> Of the full Deity possessed,
>   Eternally Divine:
> Worthy, O Lamb of God, art Thou
> That every knee to Thee should bow.
>
> True Image of the Infinite,
>   Whose essence is concealed;

Brightness of uncreated light;
    The heart of God revealed:
Worthy, O Lamb of God, art Thou
That every knee to Thee should bow.

Of all the coming endless bliss
    The Center and the Sun;
Our endless theme of praise be this,
    To Heaven's beloved One:
Worthy, O Lamb of God, art Thou
That every knee to Thee should bow.

APPENDIX

ISAIAH 53

꜅

UNDOUBTEDLY, since the advent of scientific "higher criticism," Old Testament prophecy has become much more intelligently appreciated. Gone forever is the mistaken idea that all the Old Testament prophecies were direct and exclusive predictions of events in the distant future, without any reference to the times and circumstances when they were uttered. It is now realized that for the most part they grew out of, and had their primary application to, the times and peoples amid which the prophet himself lived.

This does not detract from their supernaturalness, but it greatly clarifies their coherence and original pertinence. The mistake comes when philological critics so desupernaturalize Old Testament prophecies that they supposedly have little or nothing *but* their first and local reference.

With a certain class of Bible scholars and expositors, the attitude to Isaiah 53, as also to various other passages in the Old Testament prophets, is: "If you study the original, with a mind freed from traditional presuppositions, and apply to it the historical method of examining ancient documents, you will soon be convinced that it refers solely to the prophet's own times, and *not* to the Jesus of the future New Testament."

Is Isaiah 53 Post-Exilic?

They base their argument mainly on two grounds: (1) that the whole of Isaiah 40 to 66, whether it is the work of one writer or a composite, is a *post*-Exile product; and (2) that right through it the "Servant of Jehovah" (its recurrent central figure) is the nation *Israel.* The underlying reason for this late-dating of the poem-prophecy is to make the sufferings of Jehovah's Servant in Isaiah 53 mean more clearly the sufferings of the deported nation Israel in its Babylonian exile. With some, though not all, a further reason for their thus delimiting the Servant of Jehovah to mean *only* Israel, then and there, is to empty the prophecy of the *supernatural,* i.e., of divine *prediction.*

My own belief is that both the above assumptions are demonstrably wrong. The Babylonian exile, although often spoken of as "the seventy years exile," lasted only 51 years, i.e., from 587 to 536 B.C. at which latter date Cyrus the Persian issued his edict freeing the Jews. One of the things which deeply affected Emperor Cyrus was that he had been fore-designated by his very name in the Hebrew prophet Isaiah as Jehovah's appointed servant for that time. It certainly was no doubtfully late "prophecy" of the Exile period which so astonished Cyrus; it was the surprise that even before he was born he had been thus divinely anticipated and *named.*

That, however, is not the only evidence for the pre-Exile date of Isaiah 40-66. There is the testimony of the Septuagint, the standard version of the Hebrew Scriptures into Greek (third century B.C.), also of the book *Ecclesiasticus* (third century B.C.), also of Josephus (first century A.D.) who actually reports Cyrus's reading "the book which *Isaiah* left behind him." But for a discussion of these and other evidences,

I refer the interested reader to volume 3 in my series *Explore the Book.*

The only other evidence which need be submitted here is one which, to any unprejudiced mind, must surely be conclusive, namely: there are *quotations* from that second part of Isaiah (chapters 40-66) in other Old Testament prophets who, by general consent, are *pre*-Exile. But here again, see volume 3 of *Explore the Book.*

Suppose, however, we were momentarily to concede for argument's sake that Isaiah 40-66 was of *post*-Exile origin; even then, could we honestly believe that the sufferings of Jehovah's Servant in chapter 53 depict the sufferings of the exiled Jews? No, the suffering of those intransigent idolaters was inflicted for their own persistent infidelity and immorality, whereas the sufferings in Isaiah 53 are those of a guileless, inoffensive, nobly submissive Victim who, although he suffers under the hand of Jehovah, is nevertheless *pleasing* to Jehovah.

Even more decisive is the fact that while the sufferings of the guilty deportees in Babylon were a penalty on their *own* misdeeds, the sufferings of Jehovah's Servant in Isaiah 53 are on behalf of *others* — which is indeed their most dominant peculiarity. Furthermore, the Sufferer in Isaiah 53 is distinguished from the people of Israel by the very fact that he is substitutionarily smitten *for* them.

Added to all this is the feature that the Sufferer in Isaiah 53 is so *personalized* as to make the passage inapplicable either to the disobedient nation as a whole or to any elect group within it. Some of those who have tried to make it refer, more or less, to the Israel nation admit that in other parts of the poem-prophecy (42:1-7; 49:5-6; 50:4-10) the "Servant of Jehovah" is so personal as to make *those* parts exclusively messianic. They are so strongly individualized, in fact, that no openminded reading can take them as mere poetic personifications of the nation.

If that is true of those other parts, it is equally so in chapter

53. Especially in those verses which detail the death and burial of Jehovah's Servant, the offering of his soul for sin, and his making intercession for the transgressors, the individuality is so marked as to pass beyond any mere personification of the nation.

About the Interpretation of Prophecy

Nevertheless, let me make two things clear. First, I agree that prophecy in general (as distinct from direct prediction) has a first meaning for the times and people and circumstances in which it was first uttered or written. Second, I agree that in Isaiah 40 to 66 there is much reference to the nation Israel both directly and pictorially. I believe that the historical approach to Old Testament prophecy is sound and necessary, but it is not the *only* true approach. I am quite prepared to accept tentatively, for instance, that Psalm 2 was originally a battle song, that Psalm 45 was an epithalamium for Solomon or maybe for Jehoram, that Psalm 110 may have had contemporary connection with a Davidic war, and even that Psalm 22 may have had some strange, prior reference subsidiary to its profound fulfillment on Golgotha.

Where such contemporary connection exists as well as the culminating fulfillment in Christ, that only makes Old Testament prophecy the more wonderful, just as the Mosaic rituals and sacrifices become the more wonderful because in them there was both a *symbolic* meaning for Israel *then,* and a *typical* meaning which looked ahead through coming centuries to their grand fulfillment in Christ.

That many Old Testament prophecies *do* have a larger, ultimate fulfillment in our Lord Jesus, beyond their merely local and temporary connection, even a non-conservative critic like the late Dr. Cheyne conceded in his exposition of the Book of Jeremiah. I quote: "As a rule, the details of a prophetic description cannot be pressed; they are mainly imaginative elaborations of a great central truth or fact. Occasionally, however, regarding the prophecies in the light of Gospel times, it is almost impossible not to observe that the Spirit of Christ which was in the prophets has overruled their expressions, so that they correspond more closely to facts than could have been reasonably anticipated. Such superabundant favours to believers in inspiration occur repeatedly in the prophecies respecting Christ."

To my own mind, of course, that is a pathetically poor view of Old Testament inspiration. The Holy Spirit did much more than "overrule" expressions used by the prophets. He inspired both thoughts and words in a direct and unique way. He guided their "expressions," and in that way he certainly *did* superintend them to describe evangelical realities which were to be revealed centuries later. Moreover, that phenomenon is found in the prophetic oracles not just "occasionally" (to use Dr. Cheyne's word) but again and again, all through the prophetic books. If scholars of the purely historical approach have to concede that this far-reaching messianic element is found in *some* prophecies, then whether it occurs in *any* given passage must be determined solely on evidence.

What, then, is the principal *mark* of this bigger, messianic content in any passage where it occurs? It is that the language, ideas, and statements of the passage *unmistakably transcend* a limiting of them to lesser subjects or events around the prophet's own day. This bigger and further reach does not necessarily exclude a smaller, temporary reference at the time when the man of God wrote, but it is unmistakably too big for confinement to then. Of course, we know for certain that many such Old Testament prophecies *do* have this latent onreach by the very fact that they have had actual *fulfillment* in our Lord, and are authoritatively endorsed by the New Testament as being intendedly fulfilled in him.

Various Views of Isaiah 53

So far as Isaiah 53 is concerned, several supposed interpretations of it have been advanced by those who would deny or greatly modify its application to our Lord. Back in the third century A.D., when Origen used that chapter in debate with the Jews, *they* explained it to mean their own nation and its sufferings. That idea has been revived and popularized in our own time, not by Jewish rabbis, but by Christian teachers of the "historical approach" school.

Grotius (1583-1645) was the first Christian scholar to interpret the passage of any other than our Lord. To him it photographed the prophet Jeremiah. Others have seen in it a picture of the "godly remnant" — the *true* Israel within the *apostate* Israel. Others have seen in it good King Josiah. To still others it describes the ill-treated Hebrew prophets as a collective body. Evangelical expositors have almost uniformly interpreted it as messianic, and therefore forepicturing our Lord Jesus.

One of the most cogent arguments that the passage forepictures our Lord is that all attempts to interpret it as picturing others have failed. *Why* have they failed? It is because, although *some* clear correspondences with others than our Lord may be found in the chapter, they are heavily outweighed by wording and statements in it which simply cannot be made to fit without exegetical torture. On the contrary, *all* the wording and statements, right to the last detail, *do* fit our Lord.

Along with that, as already remarked, is the witness of the

New Testament. Wherever the Gospel or the Epistles quote or allude to Isaiah 53 they apply it clearly and solely to him. That will be sufficiently conclusive to all who accept the New Testament as having divine authority.

Somehow, from earliest times, nearly all thoughtful readers and students of Isaiah 53 have *sensed* that it had the "mark" of that bigger, messianic reference in it. The ancient rabbis of Israel, puzzled though they were how to combine such a sorrowful strain as Isaiah 53 with their jubilant messianic hope, and in spite of their strong desire to rip away the witness of Old Testament prophecy from Jesus of Nazareth, found themselves compelled to acknowledge a mysterious connection between this suffering "Servant of Jehovah" and the King-Messiah who in the latter days should gather the outcasts of Israel.

Is the Sufferer the Israel Nation?

We might comfortably dismiss the matter there were it not for the wide impression abroad nowadays that modern Old Testament scholarship has finally settled it that Isaiah 53 belongs mainly, if not wholly, to *the nation Israel.* It may be worth while to take a brief but thoughtful look again at that idea. To my own mind, it is surprising how many evangelical writers apparently feel obliged to doff their caps at that fashionable idea, and apply the chapter largely — sometimes mainly — to the suffering Jews in their Babylonian exile.

That fifty-third chapter is a part of the "Book of Consolations," as the rabbis call Isaiah 40—66 (from its opening words, "Comfort ye, comfort ye my people"). Its standpoint is supposed to be that of someone who is among, or about contemporary with, the exiled Jews in Babylonia. He sees around him the shattered wreck of his nation, a people now in the crushing grip of a Gentile despot. The corporate and political character of the elect nation seems mutilated beyond recovery. Born of this agony is the suffering prophet's message of comfort that Israel is still Jehovah's servant, and shall eventually be delivered. "Thou, Israel, art my servant; Jacob whom I have chosen; the seed of Abraham my friend. I, Jehovah, will hold thy right hand, saying unto thee: Fear not, I will help thee. This people have I formed for myself: they shall show forth my praise."

This prophet of the Exile is supposedly given to see more deeply than others into the mystery of Israel's sufferings. "Here is the elect nation, charged with a messianic function, and still bearing in its mangled bosom the mystery of redemption: here it is, passing, by God's appointment, through the deep waters of affliction. How can this baptism of suffering be other than a part of the process through which it moves onward to the fulfillment of its divine calling? What is more natural than that the wasting and agony before the prophet's eyes should shape itself, in his mind, into a sort of *redemptive passion* endured by Israel as Jehovah's chosen servant in pursuance of its divine destiny to be his channel of blessing to the world?"

"Others might cast a contemptuous glance on its misery, and be satisfied with saying that God had smitten it as its sins deserved. But to the prophet's mind, illuminated by the revealing Spirit, the suffering would assume a *vicarious* aspect, and be viewed as instrumental to the advancement of God's saving purpose. The holy nation, bowed down to the dust and trampled upon by the heathen oppressor, would appear as if agonizing in sore travail, and bringing forth in labor-pangs the universal kingdom of God."

Well, all that is vividly imaginative, but to say that the "revealing *Spirit*" put such an idea into the prophet's mind is, to me, a daring presumption. How can there be any genuine identifying of such a people, punished and exiled for idolatry, infidelity, and gross immorality, with the innocent, sinless, sublime Sufferer in Isaiah 53? To refer that chapter in any way to such an insensately wicked people, dragged into penal captivity as the inveterate betrayers of Jehovah, certainly does need imagination! Is it not strangely naive? Surely it is far more in keeping with the facts to believe that Isaiah 53 was written *before* the Exile (as was the pre-naming of Cyrus) in order to be *ready* for the Exile, so that the people, suffering for their own impenitent apostasy, should be led to repent and look away to the great Sinbearer in whom should be their ultimate salvation both as individuals and as a nation. Amid their exile, this was the one *true* "comfort," if only they would believe it, and respond to it, and return in *heart* to Jehovah.

It is equally wrong to say that exiled Israel's "baptism of suffering" was a "part of the process" in fulfillment of the nation's divine calling. No, that would make the depraving idolatry which *caused* the Exile part of the process!

It is even worse to say that the Holy Spirit "illuminated" the prophet to see in disobedient Israel's sufferings a "vicarious aspect." That is an "aspect" which those sufferings could *not* have had: for again and again God told the recalcitrant generation that they were being judged and punished for their *own* sins.

As for that further idea which is supposed to have developed in the prophet's mind, namely, that Israel in the Exile was, so to speak, "agonizing in sore travail, and bringing forth in labor-pangs the universal kingdom of God," that is indeed a big feat of imagination when one considers what the Exile actually *did* bring forth. It certainly did not "bring forth" the "kingdom of God" to fill the earth, nor by any delayed action has it done so yet, 2500 years later.

Only too willingly can I concede that the whole story of Israel, the nation of divine election, including and culminating in the Messiah, has an "ideal unity" and embodies the conception that "Israel itself in its corporate and collective capacity has a messianic character." Yet that does not give any warrant whatever for assuming that it is the *nation* which is the subject in Isaiah 53, any more than in various other passages where the language can be applied *only* to the personal Messiah himself. It is never sound exegesis to make *any* passage of Scripture "fit" to ideas imported from other passages. The interpretation of each must be decided by its own wording and other internal evidence. On the grounds of strict exegesis Isaiah 53 does *not* fit the Israel *nation*.

Inconsistent Suppositions

We must therefore disagree with the following. "Let it be remembered that in their higher and ideal character the main lines of Israel's story are *typical,* and it must be admitted that this holds good above all else in such a catastrophic event as the crushing of the nation beneath the heel of Babylon, with its subsequent exile and misery, followed by its *marvelous restoration.* If a type of the Messiah at all, Israel *must* have been a type of him here."

Thus Isaiah 53, with its substitutionary sufferings and final triumph, is supposed to have its fulfillment, or at least its primary fulfillment, in Judah's Babylonian exile and the "marvelous restoration" which followed it.

We have already shown how impossible it is to see any real likeness between the vicarious sufferings of the innocent Substitute in Isaiah 53 and the *retributive* scourging which the Babylonian exile inflicted on guilty Judah. As for the "marvelous restoration" which followed it (according to the above quotation) it was anything *but* that! When Cyrus issued his famous edict in 536 B.C., allowing all the Jews to leave for their own land, the great majority of them did not go — did not even *want* to go! A mere "remnant" of some forty-six to fifty thousand struggled back under Zerubbabel's leadership. Nor is the checkered story of that remnant any too happy, either morally or politically, during the five hundred years between then and the time of our Lord's birth in Bethlehem.

The exile in Babylon certainly cured the Jews of idolatry and made them the most rigid monotheists in history, but instead of their being changed by the "marvelous restoration" into evangelists of the "kingdom of God," they developed such bitter, relentless anti-Gentile hatred, and such isolationism, that they blinded their own minds even beyond recognizing the "kingdom" when Jesus came and offered it to them!

In that blinding hatred they even crucified their divine King, mocked and murdered his followers, and brought on themselves the fearful destruction of Jerusalem in A.D. 70.

Therefore, to see in that long-ago return of the Jewish remnant a fulfillment, or even a faint picture, of the Messiah's final triumph as worded in Isaiah 53 is even more pathetic than to see in *exiled* Judah a "primary sketch or prelusive outline" (as one writer calls it) of our Lord's Calvary sufferings.

Defective Views of Inspiration

Of course, it needs to be realized that most of those who insist on interpreting Isaiah 53 of the Israel nation have a different view of inspiration from mine. With some of them the recurring concept of "Jehovah's Servant" in Isaiah 40—66 seems scarcely more than a remarkable product of perceptive evolution in the prophet's own thinking, or in the conglomerate thinking of a plurality of contributors.

Those who hold that all those chapters (40—66) are from one writer — an anonymity whom they please to call "Deutero-Isaiah" — tell us we must bear in mind that the prophet was not writing with didactic calmness but in a "white heat of emotion and desire, of faith and hope" (a strangely different attitude from the overwhelming bulk of his earthly-minded people, who no more saw themselves or Israel as a type of some promised suffering Messiah than they saw the need of returning to their homeland when the opportunity came).

Basic to everything, modernistic scholars tell us, was the prophet's conviction that Israel was an elect and "anointed" nation, i.e., a "messianic nation," Jehovah's servant to fulfill a divine purpose toward all mankind. But amid the humiliation and wreckage of his nation in Babylonia the prophet came to see through his tears (so they say) beyond the *actual* Israel to an *ideal* Israel, a true "Servant of Jehovah," in which the purpose should be realized. "Yes, an *ideal* Israel of the future!"

Then, while he muses as to how such an ideal Israel should emerge, he rises to a yet higher, *personalized* concept. I quote: "What if the nation were to produce and culminate in one perfect 'Servant of Jehovah' through whom its vocation were to be accomplished! Other prophets had looked forward to a Davidic King reigning in righteousness and bringing peace and salvation to Israel. Why should not the same hope now take form in an individual Servant, raised up of God out of the bosom of the nation, through whose *travail* the kingdom of God should at last be born into the world?"

My own persuasion is, that any such accounting for the "Servant of Jehovah" as the excogitation of a fertile religious imagination, which the Holy Spirit, so to speak, adopted and adapted, is scarcely worth calling inspiration. In fact, it is *not* inspiration in the true and vital scriptural sense. I believe, on ample scriptural grounds, that the Holy Spirit directly revealed what he wanted those Old Testament prophets to see and to say. There was no swamping of their individuality, but there was direct, supernatural, and inerrant inspiration. What Isaiah saw and then wrote about the "Servant of Jehovah" was directly revealed to him. As I read through Isaiah's "Book of Consolations" (40—66) I am prepared to see as the "Servant of Jehovah": (1) the nation Israel in some passages, (2) an ideal Israel of the future in others, (3) the personal Messiah, our Lord Jesus Christ, in others. In each case, evidence in the passage itself must decide. All three do not coincide in any one passage. In Isaiah 53 it is neither the actual nor the ideal Israel nation which is in view. *All* the evidence is that it refers to our Lord Jesus, and to him alone.

The Popular Presentation

I do not wish to lengthen this appendix disproportionately, but let me add one further culling — from a book which was published some years ago and which presents in specious form for the general reader this newly popularized idea that the Suffering Servant of Isaiah 53 is *the nation Israel.* Its able penman is very "modern" in his approach to the four Songs of the Suffering Servant in Isaiah (42:1-4; 49:1-6; 50:4-9; 52:13—53:12). While apparently accepting the "bulk" of chapters 40 to 55 as written by the so-called "Deutero-Isaiah," he tells us approvingly that some scholars believe the four songs to be insertions from another hand.

Some of us wonder with solemn awe at the confidence with which those scholars can detect changes of authorship in this and that and the other paragraph, and dissect the Book of Isaiah into the many fragments which together, supposedly, form the total mosaic called "Isaiah." Often a detailed comparison of the segments shows that the asserted differences of vocabulary, style, background, etc., which are supposed to indicate different authors, are fanciful rather than factual. Over against the doubtful *dis*similarities are the far more patent *similarities* which betoken the unity of the whole book from the one, well-known prophet Isaiah of Hezekiah's time.

The modern author of the publication which we now quote represents many preachers in our main Protestant denominations. He writes as follows.

"Israel is to be restored with this larger purpose in view, to bring all men to the truth of God. . . . In the third Song the insults and cruelties which the Servant has had to endure are mentioned. In spite of everything he maintains his confidence in Jehovah his Instructor and is certain that the time of his vindication is at hand. The fourth Song (Isaiah 53) describes this vindication: just as many had been astonished at his sufferings, so shall they be startled by the glory that shall be given him. Even kings shall be hushed to silence at so great a transformation: the nations will exclaim, 'Who would have believed it? For *Israel* was a thing of no account; men even turned away in revulsion from so despised a nation. We thought that the Servant's sufferings were God's punishment for his sins, but now we recognize that it was *our* sins that caused his pain. It was to win peace for *us* that he suffered chastisement. For we (i.e., Gentiles) like sheep had gone astray, and needed to be rescued. And in all that he endured he made no complaint, even when he, although innocent, was stricken to death [a supposed reference to Israel's loss of national existence in the "death" of the Exile!]. And then Jehovah delivered him, and gave him a position of great exaltation. . . .' The literature of the Exile is full of this hope of better days to be; days of national restoration and of spiritual and moral transformation."

The contradictions in such an interpretation of Isaiah 53 are so glaring as scarcely to need pointing out. To say of that stiff-necked generation of obdurate offenders, ejected from Canaan into humiliating retribution, that "in spite of everything he maintains his confidence in Jehovah his Instructor, and is certain that the time of his vindication is at hand," makes a travesty either of Bible prophecy or of some modern scholarship.

It is egregiously worse to make out that the nation's sufferings were not for its own sins but the sins of *other nations,* so that at last the Gentile nations say, "We thought that the Servant's sufferings were God's punishment for his sins, but now we recognize that it was *our* sins that caused his pain; it was to win peace for *us* that he suffered chastisement. For we like sheep had gone astray and needed to be rescued"!

What God *actually* says through Isaiah is that it was *Israel* which had gone astray (the "all *we*" in verse 6 is Isaiah the *Jew* speaking as being one with his own *Jewish* people, as is confirmed by verse 8, "For the transgression of *my* people . . ." i.e., the covenant people).

As for the return from the Exile being the "vindication" and "transformation" of the Servant, we have shown already how absurd that idea is. Not only did a mere handful return, comparatively speaking, but they came back to wrecked cities and silted debris, as a vassal people with no longer any king or throne or independent government of their own. Their fortunes were henceforth tossed about by successive ruling powers. Only once was there a short interval of tenuous independence (part of the Maccabean period: 163-67 B.C.). Then came subjection to imperial Rome, followed in A.D. 70 by the fearful *climax* of that post-Exile period, the still deadlier destruction of Jerusalem, and a worldwide further scattering of Jews which has lasted until present times. Yet we are asked to believe that this was the foreseen "vindication" and "transformation"! It would seem as though some people will swallow anything rather than accept the traditional and supernaturalist view of the Bible.

Israel: the Actual versus the Ideal

However, the author of the above-quoted book must have had some secret discomfort about his interpretation of the "Servant" in Isaiah 53, for he goes on to bring him into focus as being the "ideal" Israel (though no such phantom has ever *yet* suffered and fulfilled Isaiah 53!). He tells us that the "Second Isaiah" now sees "with truly amazing spiritual insight . . . that the very sufferings of the nation have their place in this great redemptive purpose. *If only* the actual Israel will act as the *ideal* Israel whom he [Deutero-Isaiah] portrays in the Songs of the Suffering Servant; if only the real Israel in exile will accept suffering without complaint or bitterness, then the very sorrows themselves will lead to the exaltation of the nation as the faithful steward of the salvation of God for all mankind."

That, pathetically enough, reduces Isaiah 53 to a wishful "if only" appeal to the obdurate nation, instead of direct divine prediction of something predetermined.

Even then the author is obliged to add, "Alas, the nation failed to rise to the challenge and call of this noble teaching. In all history *only One* has done so." Why then does not our modern author come right out and agree that Isaiah 53 is a direct prediction pointing on through the centuries to that *"only One"* in all history who fulfils it? Apparently it is just because he is a bit too modern. He says, "The prophet *discerned* a spiritual truth which only Jesus has fulfilled. That is why, for centuries, some have taken this part of his prophecy as a direct foretelling of the coming of our Lord Jesus Christ."

To my own mind, that author has a pretty poor concept of biblical inspiration (that is nearly always the trouble) when he says that Isaiah 53 was merely something which "the prophet *discerned.*" My own view is that it was something which

God directly *revealed,* for in verses 11 and 12 it is God himself speaking: "By his knowledge shall *my* righteous servant justify many," etc. It *cannot* be merely that the prophet "discerned a spiritual truth," for he describes centuries in advance, and in remarkable detail, the submission, sufferings, death, and ultimate post-mortem triumph of the most wonderful Being who ever came into human history.

So decidedly do the description and details fit *him,* and him exclusively, that for Christian expositors to insist on bending them into any other direction not only impoverishes the prophecy, but seems almost an irreverent impertinence to clear-worded divine revelation.

Why It Cannot Mean the Nation

To sum up, we submit six reasons-in-brief why the Suffering Servant of Isaiah 53 cannot be the nation Israel.

1. The singular personal *pronouns* "he," "him," "his" in this chapter *separate* the Sufferer from the Israel nation, for the nation speaks in the plurals, "we" and "our" and "us" in verses 4, 5, 6. Furthermore, those plurals cannot be the *Gentile* nations addressing the Israel nation, because they are ascribed to Israel ("my people," verse 8).

2. The sufferings of Jehovah's Servant in Isaiah 53 are *vicarious,* as is corroborated again and again in other parts of Scripture, whereas the Israel nation's sufferings were penal and corrective, as is stated repeatedly in Scripture, without the faintest suggestion anywhere that they were otherwise.

3. The Sufferer in Isaiah 53 suffers vicariously *for* the nation, so he cannot very well *be* the nation on behalf of which he substitutionarily suffers.

4. He suffers both voluntarily and submissively without complaint or resistance. That is far from true of the Israel *nation,* as everyone knows. For centuries after the Exile the Jews broke out in fierce, desperate insurrections, nor did these cease even with the butchery and scattering of them from Judea in A.D. 70. Their hatred, not only of the Romans, but of *all* the Gentiles was proverbial. Right up to the seventh century of our Christian era these revolts periodically occurred.

5. The sufferings of the innocent Victim in Isaiah 53 ended in *death and burial.* That is the very opposite of what is foretold again and again of Israel's sufferings as a nation. No earthly power shall stamp out the Jews. No scattering, however prolonged, shall extinguish them. At the same time as they are punished they shall be preserved, and most certainly in the end they shall be regathered. See passages such as Jeremiah 30:11; 31:35-38; 33:20, 21; Isaiah 11 and 12; Ezekiel 11:16-20; Psalm 89:28-37; Romans 11:1, 2, 25-29.

6. The sufferings in Isaiah 53 were personally undeserved and were borne by One whom Jehovah himself calls, "My *righteous* Servant" (v. 11), which at once separates the Sufferer from the nation against which Jehovah alleges the very opposite of righteousness over and over again.

Why It Cannot Mean the "Godly Remnant"

But if the Suffering Servant is not the nation Israel, is he the *"godly remnant"* personified — the faithful few among the impenitent many? That is an alternate view held fairly widely. Here are six reasons which to me seem valid and cogent why Isaiah 53 cannot refer to the "godly remnant."

1. The sufferings in Isaiah 53 are inflicted by *Jehovah himself* (vv. 6, 10). One of the sad ironies of history is that through social complexity the innocent all too often suffer with the guilty in some general calamity brought on by the wicked. But it is simply unthinkable that God himself would directly inflict punishment and death on an innocent minority *instead of* on the guilty. Yet that is what Isaiah 53 would teach if the Sufferer were the godly remnant in Israel.

2. If the Sufferer in Isaiah 53 is the godly remnant in Israel, then godly *Isaiah* is made to place himself, not with *them,* but with the *un*godly who went "astray" and "turned everyone to his own way," for he includes himself in the "our" and "we" and "us" of verses 4, 5, 6. Isaiah thus separates himself from the godly remnant and becomes one of the "despisers" (verse 3), if the Sufferer is the godly remnant!

3. Some of the *wording* simply will not fit any such "godly remnant" — e.g., being buried "with the rich" (v. 9); the "pleasure of Jehovah *prospering*" in their hand (v. 10) when the very opposite has been the case; the being regarded as "afflicted of God" (v. 4) — for the ungodly in Israel *never* so regarded the godly: they knew well enough that it was they themselves (not God) who afflicted the godly.

4. The most startling peculiarity of the Servant's sufferings is that they were *vicariously atoning.* Will any of us dare to say that the persecutions of the godly by the ungodly in Israel were either vicarious or atoning? Sin, basically, is rebellious disobedience and transgression against an infinite God, and requires infinite reparation. One has only to reflect on this to realize that substitutionary atonement such as is indicated in verses 5, 6, and 10 is utterly beyond any merely human group. Moreover, even the godliest humans are still sinners themselves. No human being can make atonement even for

his or her own sin, let alone for the vast guilt-aggregate of the many!

5. The sufferings of Jehovah's righteous Servant in Isaiah 53 terminated in death and burial. In the words of verse 8, he was *"cut off* out of the land of the living." That is not true of the godly remnant. As a group they are to persist right on to the future consummation. They will *never* be "cut off"; Jehovah will always have his loyal inner circle within Israel. See, for instance, the "seven thousand" in 1 Kings 19:18 who had not "bowed the knee to Baal," with Paul's comment in Romans 11:5; also Malachi 3:16, 17, Ezekiel 9:4, and the 144,000 of Revelation 7 and 14. The One who *was* "cut off" out of the land of the living, as in Isaiah 53, was Israel's *Messiah,* of whom we read in Daniel 9:26, "And after threescore and two weeks shall Messiah be *cut off. . . ."*

6. Isaiah 53:11 says, "By his knowledge shall my righteous Servant justify many, for he shall bear their iniquities." More recent translations are helpful in bringing out the full meaning: "Through the knowledge of himself (by others) my righteous Servant shall obtain righteousness for the many." So there, away back in the Old Testament, as clear as can be, is the doctrine of justification through the imputed righteousness of a substitutionary Sin-bearer. Let it be said with categorical decisiveness, no "godly remnant" ever did, ever could, or ever will bear sin and provide justification for others in that way. That the perverted majority in old-time Israel or the majority at any other time, present or future, should be exonerated, excused, or in any way justified by the suffering of the "godly remnant" is an idea which cannot be entertained for one moment.

The One True Fulfillment

Finally, here are twelve fulfillments of Isaiah 53 in our Lord Jesus which confirm that he is the one and only figure in all history who obviously and completely answers to all the requirements of the prophecy.

1. He came of the lowliest human stock, answering to verse 2: a "root out of a dry ground."

2. He was despised as the Nazarene of mean birth, in line with verse 3: "despised and rejected of men."

3. He suffered for sins in the place of others, as he himself taught (Matt. 20; 28, etc.), thus fulfilling verses 4, 5 and 6: "wounded for *our* transgressions" etc.

4. He was actually "delivered up" (Rom. 8:32) by God the Father (Acts 2:23) thus strikingly answering to the words of Isaiah 53:10, "It pleased Jehovah to bruise him."

5. He submitted with uncomplaining, utter resignation, thus sublimely implementing verse 7: "He was oppressed, and he was afflicted, yet he opened not his mouth. . . ."

6. He was executed as a felon between two outlaws, thus bringing to pass verse 8, "taken from prison and judgment"; and verse 9, "made his grave with the wicked."

7. He was cut off prematurely, in his early thirties, and in sudden abortion of his impact on the people, thereby fitting the wording of verse 8, "cut off out of the land of the living."

8. He was personally guiltless and guileless, so much so that his accusers contradicted and confounded themselves, and could

only charge, falsely, the utterance of blasphemy, which was exactly as foretold in verse 9, "He had done no violence, neither was any deceit in his mouth."

9. He was to live on (strange as the prophecy seemed) even after his sufferings and death, according to verse 10, "He shall see his seed [or followers]; he shall prolong his days." This seeming enigma suddenly began to be unlocked when Jesus rose from the grave in resurrection life.

10. He thus began to unloose the meaning of those further words in verse 10, "The pleasure of Jehovah shall prosper in his hand."

11. As the risen Victor he declared, "All authority is given unto me in heaven and on earth"; and the whole New Testament rings with his victory and exaltation, and with the hope of his second advent in glory and global empire. What abundant and unique fulfillment of verse 12: "Therefore will I divide him his portion with the great, and he shall divide the spoil with the strong"!

12. By all this, and by "justifying many," and saving a "multitude which no man can number" he gives everlasting fulfillment to the words of verse 11, "He shall see of the travail of his soul, and shall be satisfied."

As trait after trait swings into focus and fulfillment, can we write any other name under Isaiah's amazing portrait of the sublime Sufferer in chapter 53 than *Jesus of Nazareth?* And can we fail to marvel at the miracle of inspiration in this prophetic anticipation of the lovely "Man of Sorrows" when we reflect that it was written some seven hundred years B.C.?

Other Books in the Living Studies Series

Apostles' Creed, The, J. I. Packer. A phrase-by-phrase explanation of the creed on which our faith in Christ rests. Six sessions.

Building People Through a Caring, Sharing Fellowship, Donald Bubna and Sarah Ricketts. Practical steps your church can take to develop koinonia fellowship and friendship evangelism. Thirteen sessions.

Colossians: A Portrait of Christ, Dr. James T. Draper, Jr. A study of how the early church dealt with false cults, intellectual elitism, and apathy. Thirteen sessions.

Discover Joy: Studies in Philippians, Dr. James T. Draper, Jr. A study of how Christians can face any situation with delight instead of despair. Thirteen sessions.

Discover Your Spiritual Gift and Use It, Rick Yohn. An examination of the relevancy and necessity of spiritual gifts in the life of every Christian. Thirteen sessions.

Dynamic Praying for Exciting Results, Russ Johnston with Maureen Rank. Christians have access to God's resources for life's demands. Thirteen sessions.

Effective Christian Ministry, Ronald W. Leigh. Principles of Christian influence based both on the Bible and on findings from the fields of psychology, sociology, and education. Thirteen sessions.

Faith that Works: Studies in James, Dr. James T. Draper, Jr. The Apostle James wrote not just a theological treatise but a message about how to live, to work, to speak, to demonstrate faith. Thirteen sessions.

Family: God's Handiwork, The, John Williams. Put aside what psychologists and sociologists have said about the family and look at what the Bible itself has to say. Thirteen sessions.

Family: Stronger After Crisis, The, Paul Welter. Conflict, anxiety, and depression become stepping stones for individual and family restoration and growth. Thirteen sessions.

Famous Couples of the Bible, Richard Strauss. A look at the marriages of the Bible shows how to strengthen your own. Good for a couples' class study. Thirteen sessions.

God in Three Persons, E. Calvin Beisner. The word trinity doesn't appear in the Bible, yet Christians hold it as a biblical truth. A study of how the doctrine was formulated. Six sessions.

Handbook to Happiness, Dr. Charles R. Solomon. A professionally trained psychologist gives a Bible-based approach to solving contemporary personal crises. Thirteen sessions.

Hidden Art of Homemaking, The, Edith Schaeffer. Many opportunities for artistic expression can be found in ordinary, everyday life. How to make any home a center of meaningful living and personal enrichment. Thirteen sessions.

His Name Is Wonderful, Warren W. Wiersbe. Isaiah's power-packed descriptions of Christ have crucial and practical meaning for us today. A study of Christ in Isaiah. Thirteen sessions.

How Come It's Taking Me So Long?, Lane Adams. A book to help new and growing Christians to understand the process of Christian growth. Thirteen sessions.

How to Get What You Pray For, Dr. Bill Austin. A study of how Christians can achieve greater success in prayer once they learn how to put themselves in harmony with the essential agents of prayer. Thirteen sessions.

How to Help a Friend, Paul Welter. A study designed to teach Christians how to discover a friend's "living channels," and tips on expressing warmth, identifying needs, and responding to crises. Thirteen sessions.

How to Really Know the Will of God, Richard Strauss. Practical suggestions for decision making discovered in God's Word. Thirteen sessions.

Leadership Life-style, Ajith Fernando. A clear examination of leadership training found in Paul's letters to Timothy. Thirteen sessions.

Listen! Jesus Is Praying, Warren W. Wiersbe. A verse-by-verse commentary on Christ's High Priestly Prayer in John 17 with practical applications. Thirteen sessions.

Live Up to Your Faith: Studies in Titus, James T. Draper, Jr. Christianity is more than right doctrines. Paul's message concerned both right believing and right living. Thirteen sessions.

Man Overboard, Sinclair B. Ferguson. A study of the life of Jonah. Not a story of a great fish but of a great God who deals with those who struggle with obedience. Six sessions.

Marriage Is for Love, Dr. Richard Strauss. An insightful look at God's principles of happy marriage. A study to strengthen the fabric of your marriage. Thirteen sessions.

Parents, Take Charge! Perry L. Draper. A psychologist explains important principles on child-rearing found in God's Word. Thirteen sessions.

Passport to the Bible, Bobi Hromas. Five minutes a day of Bible study and the Word comes alive. Bible study methods and dozens of ways to read, understand, and apply Bible truth. Thirteen sessions.

Proverbs: Practical Directions for Living, James T. Draper, Jr. A book to help people get a handle on studying Proverbs. Thirteen sessions.

Reality of Hell and the Goodness of God, The, Harold T. Bryson. A study of the biblical doctrine of hell and how it is consistent with a good and gracious God. Six sessions.

Run with the Winners, Warren W. Wiersbe. A study of Hebrews 11 and the "Hall of Fame of Faith." Defines biblical faith and how it works. Thirteen sessions.

Self-Control, Russell Kelfer. A study of the enemies of self-control—the attitudes, appetites, and activities that threaten to control our lives. Thirteen sessions.

Sex Roles and the Christian Family, W. Peter Blitchington. There is a specific pattern for family relationships designed by God and set in motion for our benefit. Thirteen sessions.

Spirit-Controlled Temperament, Dr. Tim LaHaye. A guide to understanding your God-given personality strengths and what the Holy Spirit can do to overcome your weaknesses. Thirteen sessions.

Standing on the Rock: The Importance of Biblical Inerrancy, James Montgomery Boice. A study outlining the current controversy and the importance of accepting the Bible as inerrant. Six sessions.

Ten Commandments, The, J. I. Packer. God in love gave us not only the gospel but the law. A study of God's moral absolutes. Six sessions.

What the Faith Is All About, Elmer L. Towns. A layman's approach to Bible doctrine that provides the solid content for the development of believers. Fifty-two sessions.

What To Do Till the Lord Comes: Studies in 1 & 2 Thessalonians, Dr. James T. Draper, Jr. A relevant message to the church trying to remain faithful amidst opposition. Thirteen sessions.